THOUGHT IN ENGLISH PROSE

THOUGHT IN ENGLISH PROSE

BY
J. C. DENT

HEADMASTER
CITY OF WESTMINSTER
SCHOOL, LONDON

WITH AN INTRODUCTION BY
WARNER TAYLOR

PROFESSOR OF ENGLISH
UNIVERSITY OF WISCONSIN

THE ODYSSEY PRESS
NEW YORK

CONTENTS

INTRODUCTION

It used to be a favorite saying of one of the oldest and sagest teachers in America that undergraduates of the present generation could not read. The printed page was there, but the will to master it lay in shadow. He placed the reason for this against the time we live in. He himself had been reared under the exacting classics. Latin and Greek had trained him to put words and phrases under the microscope, to scrutinize them with a scholar's nicety, to deal with them justly and finely. The half century of his university teaching watched the passing of Virgil and Homer. It witnessed, too, such a scattering of under-graduate preoccupations—with the social and the athletic walking abreast of the mental—that the former unity of purpose lost its sharp edges. It saw a simple curriculum grow Hydra-headed and many-limbed, looking all ways at once, and with its reach exceeding its grasp. In the old days there was no philandering with Latin prose or poetry; you made love to it or you did not win it. Translation either from or into the original demanded "the one word for the one thing," the *mot juste* of Flaubert. The classics developed the habit of close observation and concentration. Students could read then. Today, I believe teach-ers of English, at least, are in agreement that they cannot. It is, therefore, with genuine interest that one turns to a volume like the present, the obvious purpose of which is to compel those who study it to grant it the forgotten cour-tesy of sustained attention.

The most securely entrenched textbook in Freshman English courses, waiving the handbook and the rhetoric, is the essay collection. About two decades ago essay anthologies began to appear regularly. Their ascent into popularity was rapid. Those first issued drew their material from the "classic" essayists; Newman, Huxley, Arnold, and their serious-minded kindred, who were studied both for style and for content. Then came a change. Contemporary essays, formal and informal, crept in; and the study of style crept out. And now many current collections are based on light, contemporary articles from yesterday's magazines. They interest and amuse students and are easy of class administration,— pleasant to read, pleasant to teach—with summer's gaiety about them. But as for discipline and the evolvement of a stern training for the mind, they play court jester to the king. Some one once said that the rich man will do anything for the poor man except get off his back; and oftentimes the teacher of an essay will do anything conceivable for that essay except teach it. There is a tendency to rest content after the general ideas have been touched upon and their application to life more or less discussed.

But surely one obligation resting squarely on Freshman English, especially in an easy-going age, is to teach students to read. It requires patience and a technique to do this. If, however, one takes the point of view towards his teaching that mental discipline is essential, he will not rest content with episodic classroom debates on the general issues of an essay; he will demand a probing, sustained analysis—the meanings of words and phrases, the references and allusions, the definite relationship of parts to whole, the functions of the particular beginning and conclusion—the acquisition of a sound and ready knowledge of all those aspects of the essay in hand that prove him an honest workman. The average student is not committed by his heritage or his environment to a more generous bestowal of his time than he is called upon to give. I dare say no teacher of English prose has ever lived who has not, on occasion, stood appalled at the lack of cleanly cut student information on seemingly obvious points in a text, at a lack of incisiveness and certainty. Answers so often have no more sharp outlines than a piece of fur.

This little volume of Mr. Dent's is designed to offer an antidote for fuzziness. His title is lucidly descriptive—*Thought in English Prose*. It means business. For the student it will—to his ultimate benefit, I should say—entail thought *on* English prose. He will find himself under the unequivocal obligation of a series of searching queries that get to the roots and fibers of the piece of prose assigned. These questions are decidedly ingenious. Many of them call for purely informational answers, but many others, most, indeed, draw on the imaginative, deductive, and aesthetic faculties. There is something of uncompromising pedagogy in all this. It assumes a need for further discipline among those who are taught, and a willingness to surrender an easy-chair attitude by those who teach. Even if one could take for granted the existence of an eager spirit for learning in an institution, the book would still be useful, for the questions themselves would serve a student as a test of the extent of his knowledge, his ingenuity, and his good taste. They would do for an undergraduate what the "*Que-sais-je?*", the "What do I really know?" of the self-examining Montaigne did for him: put him in possession of his stock of facts. And these questions on text do not seem petty or finical to me: they keep to the heart of the affair. Nor do they involve matters of style as such. Perhaps this is just as well where so many instructors hold against putting subtle effects on the operating table, scraping the chromatic scales from butterflies' wings.

Mr. Dent himself, in suggesting a possible procedure to be followed under his method, states: "Most of the exercises proposed in this book can be prepared privately by the student and worked through orally in class. But the following method of study is recommended. The passage should be read through aloud by teacher or by student. Then should follow at least three private readings by the student before any of the questions are attempted. These questions are so arranged that they will, for the most part, take the student consecutively through the passage. Above all, there should be no haste." Mr. Dent, in other words, proposes that the extracts be *studied*, a performance in polar antithesis to that employed in summer hammock reading where the high spots are hit with speed and certainty by a luxurious mind on the defensive against serious effort.

Again he states: "Dr. Johnson said long ago that questioning is not the mode of conversation among gentlemen, and one has the feeling that a series of questions such as are to be found in this book is a painfully mechanical attempt to approach the beauty and power of English expression." Later, "No intelligent teacher will suppose that the only way to read English prose is indicated in this book . . . And yet in these days, when so many voices are clamoring to be heard, and so many charlatans are exploiting a popular Press, it cannot be unprofitable to draw the attention of young students to some of the principles upon which the practice of English prose depends, to point out the subtleties that may underlie an apparently simple statement, and to put them on their guard against mistaking a hazy conception for a knowledge that rests upon a sure foundation." What Mr. Dent does maintain is that his method is one method. That it happens to be proved by time and logic, allows a teacher sympathetic to the procedure to administer the book with a large degree of confidence.

WARNER TAYLOR

University of Wisconsin
April, 1930

THOUGHT IN ENGLISH PROSE

No. I

1. For the rest of the day we saw no human being; we pushed on eagerly in the hope of coming up with the Bedouins before nightfall. Night came, and we still went on in our way till about ten o'clock. Then the thorough darkness of the night, and the weariness of our beasts (they had already done two good days' journey in one), forced us to determine upon coming to a standstill. Upon the heights to the eastward we saw lights; these shone from caves on the mountainside, inhabited, as the Nazarene told us, by rascals of a low sort—not real Bedouins—men whom we might frighten into harmlessness, but from whom there was no willing hospitality to be expected.

2. We heard at a little distance the brawling of a rivulet, and on the banks of this it was determined to establish our bivouac; we soon found the stream, and following its course for a few yards came to a spot which was thought to be fit for our purpose. It was a sharply cold night in February, and when I dismounted, I found myself standing upon some wet, rank herbage that promised ill for the comfort of our resting-place. I had bad hopes of a fire, for the pitchy darkness of the night was a great obstacle to any successful search for fuel, and besides, the boughs of trees or bushes would be so full of sap in this early spring, that they would not easily burn. However, we were not likely to submit to a dark and cold bivouac without an effort, and my fellows groped forward through the darkness till, after advancing a few paces, they were

1

happily stopped by a complete barrier of dead prickly
bushes. Before our swords could be drawn to reap this
30 welcome harvest, it was found to our surprise that the fuel
was already hewn, and strewed along the ground in a thick
mass. A spot for the fire was found with some difficulty,
for the earth was moist, and the grass high and rank.
At last there was a clicking of flint and steel, and presently
35 there stood out from darkness one of the tawny faces of
my muleteers, bent down to near the ground, and suddenly
lit up by the glowing of the spark, which he courted with
careful breath. Before long there was a particle of dry
fiber or leaf that kindled to a tiny flame; then another
40 was lit from that, and then another. Then small, crisp
twigs, little bigger than bodkins, were laid athwart the
glowing fire. The swelling cheeks of the muleteer, laid
level with the earth, blew tenderly at first, then more
boldly, and the young flame was daintily nursed and fed,
45 and fed more plentifully till it gained good strength. At
last a whole armful of dry bushes was piled up over the
fire, and presently, with a loud, cheery cracking and
crackling, a royal tall blaze shot up from the earth, and
showed me once more the shapes and faces of my men,
50 and the dim outlines of the horses and mules that stood
grazing hard by.

3. My servants busied themselves in unpacking the
baggage, as though we had arrived at an hotel—Shereef
and his helpers unsaddled their cattle. We had left
55 Tiberias without the slightest idea that we were to make
our way to Jerusalem along the desolate side of the Jordan,
and my servants (generally provident in those matters)
had brought with them only, I think, some unleavened
bread, and a rocky fragment of goat's-milk cheese.
60 These treasures were produced. Tea, and the contrivances
for making it, were always a standing part of my baggage.
My men gathered in a circle round the fire. The Nazarene
was in a false position, from having misled us so strangely,

and he would have shrunk back, poor devil, into the cold
and outer darkness, but I made him draw near, and share 65
the luxuries of the night.   My quilt and my pelisse were
spread, and the rest of my people had all their capotes or
pelisses, or robes of some sort, which furnished their
couches.   The men gathered in circle, some kneeling, some
sitting, some lying reclined around our common hearth. 70
Sometimes on one, sometimes on another, the flickering
light would glare more fiercely.   Sometimes it was the
good Shereef that seemed the foremost, as he sat with
venerable beard, the image of manly piety—unknowing
of all geography, unknowing where he was, or whither he 75
might go, but trusting in the goodness of God, and the
clenching power of fate, and the good star of the Englishman.   Sometimes, like marble, the classic face of the
Greek Mysseri would catch the sudden light, and then
again, by turns, the ever-perturbed Dthemetri, with his 80
odd Chinaman's eye, and bristling terrier-like moustache,
shone forth illustrious.

WILLIAM KINGLAKE

QUESTIONS

1. Give a title to this extract.
2. Give titles to the paragraphs.
3. What is the key-sentence of the first paragraph?[1]
4. Lights to the eastward—caves on the mountainside—
   rascals of a low sort—frighten into harmlessness—no
   willing hospitality. Of these phrases, which for the
   purposes of the whole extract is the most important?
   Why?
5. What is the key-sentence to the second paragraph?

[1]The word "sentence" is used throughout the questions in this book
to indicate a grammatically independent group of words containing subject and predicate, and NOT necessarily all the words between two full
stops.

6. Divide the second paragraph into four sections:

    (a) Discovery.

    (b) Despondency.

    (c) Luck.

    (d) Achievement.

    Indicate these sections, and substitute for the titles given above a short phrase (the shorter the better) taken from each of the sections.

7. In describing the lighting of the fire (the passage begins, "At last there was a clicking . . .") Kinglake appeals first to our sense of hearing. *dark nite   scary*

    (a) Why is this so effective in this context? *neat all*

    In the next sentence he appeals to our sense of sight. But he does not say, "I saw one of the tawny faces." If he had done so, the ideas of —ness and of —ness would have been lost. *darkness, brightness*

    (b) Complete the —ness words.

8. Write down phrases in the second paragraph by means of which Kinglake shows us that vision was at first only partial.

9. What words does Kinglake use to indicate delicate action in lighting the fire?

*spark
flame
spot,*

10. After the striking of flint and steel there are five steps to be marked in the progress of the fire. Indicate those steps by five phrases taken from Kinglake's description. No phrase should consist of more than four words, and most of them need only two words.

11. What is the essential difference between "glow" and "flame"?

12. What would be the loss in effect if "with a loud cheery cracking and crackling" were omitted?

13. Why is "royal" such an excellent epithet in this context (l.48)?

14. There are three general statements (a, b, c), in the third paragraph, which, written consecutively, will give the gist of the whole paragraph. What are they?

15. How does Kinglake expand these general statements? You are not asked to write down the sentences in which Kinglake does this; you are asked to indicate very briefly the method: thus—"He expands the general statement a by——."

16.   (a) In place of "treasures" (l. 60) what word might Kinglake have used having the same derivation as a word in the preceding sentence? *provisions*

    (b) Had he done so he would have lost an idea. What is it? *value of their scantiness*

    (c) What other word in the paragraph suggests the same idea? *luxuries afforded*

17. What is the exact meaning of "furnished" (l.68)?

18. What does Kinglake mean by "the good star of the Englishman" (l. 77)? *England had ruled for several centuries. British Emp.*

19. Why is the power of fate called "clenching"?

20. "The goodness of God, and the clenching power of fate, and the good star of the Englishman." At least one reader of Kinglake is always inclined to smile when he reads this passage and considers the order in which the phrases are arranged. If you share his sense of humor try to explain what it is that provokes the smile. *that he includes England with fate and God. Most & thing last*

21. "Sometimes the flickering light would reveal Mysseri sitting like ——." Supply a simile that will embody the ideas of marble—classic—Greek.

22.   (a) Shereef: venerable—pious—trusting.

    (b) Mysseri: marble—classic—Greek.

    (c) Dthemetri: ever-perturbed—bustling—terrier-like. *scurrying*
    Each group of words should call up a general impression. Supply for each group one adjective that will suggest the impression.

23. Why is "illustrious" such an aptly chosen word in this passage? *providing for the future / sermon at-guard = camp for a night*

24. Give the derivation and meaning (in this passage) of— determine — bivouac — obstacle — tawny — daintily — fragment—provident—classic. *brussels saving   obstare- to stand in the way   tanneic* *strange! part*

25. Learn by heart the passage "At last there was a clicking . . . grazing hard by." *typical; traditional; endures; Gr. x.   diagraphs   worth, dignity*

26. "It was decided, in spite of some opposition, that if an entry could be effected, the chemical laboratory would be an excellent place for the feast." Expand this into a paragraph along the following lines. *neoclassic- revival of classical arts   omit*

    (a) Grounds of opposition. (What *are* the objections to eating food in such a place?)

    (b) Difficulty of entry.

(c) Details of the menu.

End your paragraph with a passage "And so, just after midnight . . ." (Continue the passage by mentioning those present, adding a few vivid touches of description.)

No. II

1. Drake began to realize that he was now entirely alone, and had only himself and his own crew to depend on. There was nothing to do but to go through with it, danger adding to the interest. Arica was the next point visited.
5 Half a hundred blocks of silver were picked up at Arica. After Arica came Lima, the chief depôt of all, where the grandest haul was looked for. At Lima, alas! they were just too late. Twelve great hulks lay anchored there. The sails were unbent, the men were ashore. They contained
10 nothing but some chests of reals and a few bales of silk and linen. But a thirteenth, called by the gods *Our Lady of the Conception*, called by men *Cacafuego*, a name incapable of translation, had sailed a few days before for the isthmus, with the whole produce of the Lima mines
15 for the season. Her ballast was silver, her cargo gold and emeralds and rubies. Drake deliberately cut the cables of the ships in the roads, that they might drive ashore and be unable to follow him. The *Pelican* spread her wings, every feather of them, and sped in pursuit. He would
20 know the *Cacafuego*, so he learnt at Lima, by the peculiar cut of her sails. The first man who caught sight of her was promised a gold chain for his reward. A sail was seen on the second day. It was not the chase, but it was worth stopping for. Eighty pounds' worth of gold was found,
25 and a great gold crucifix, set with emeralds said to be as large as pigeons' eggs. They took the kernel. They left the shell. Still on and on. We learn from the Spanish

accounts that the Viceroy of Lima, as soon as he recovered
from his astonishment, dispatched ships in pursuit. They
came up with the last plundered vessel, heard terrible 30
tales of the rovers' strength, and went back for a larger
force. The *Pelican* meanwhile went along upon her course
for eight hundred miles. At length, when in the latitude
of Quito and close under the shore, the *Cacafuego's* peculiar
sails were sighted, and the gold chain was claimed. There 35
she was, freighted with the fruit of Aladdin's garden, going
lazily along a few miles ahead. Care was needed in ap-
proaching her. If she guessed the *Pelican's* character,
she would run in upon the land and they would lose her.
It was afternoon. The sun was still above the horizon, 40
and Drake meant to wait till night, when the breeze would
be off the shore, as in the tropics it always is.

2. The *Pelican* sailed two feet to the *Cacafuego's* one.
Drake filled his empty wine-skins with water and trailed
them astern to stop his way. The chase supposed that she 45
was followed by some heavy-loaded trader, and, wishing
for company on a lonely voyage, she slackened sail and
waited for him to come up. At length the sun went down
into the ocean, the rosy light faded from off the snows of
the Andes; and when both ships had become invisible 50
from the shore, the skins were hauled in, the night wind
rose, and the water began to ripple under the *Pelican's*
bows. The *Cacafuego* was swiftly overtaken, and when
within a cable's length a voice hailed her to put her head
into the wind. The Spanish commander, not understand- 55
ing so strange an order, held on his course. A broadside
brought down his mainyard, and a flight of arrows rattled
on his deck. He was himself wounded. In a few minutes
he was a prisoner, and *Our Lady of the Conception* and her
precious freight were in the corsair's power. The wreck 60
was cut away; the ship was cleared; a prize crew was
put on board. Both vessels turned their heads to the sea.
At daybreak no land was to be seen, and the examination

of the prize began.   The full value was never acknowledged.
65 The invoice, if there was one, was destroyed.   The accurate
figures were known only to Drake and Queen Elizabeth.
A published schedule acknowledged to twenty tons of
silver bullion, thirteen chests of silver coins, and a hundred-
weight of gold, but there were gold nuggets besides in
70 indefinite quantity, and "a great store" of pearls, emeralds, and diamonds.   The Spanish Government proved a
loss of a million and a half of ducats, excluding what
belonged to private persons.   The total capture was
immeasurably greater.

75   3. Drake, we are told, was greatly satisfied.   He thought
it prudent to stay in the neighborhood no longer than
necessary.   He went north with all sail set, taking his
prize along with him.   The master, San Juan de Anton,
was removed on board the *Pelican* to have his wound
80 attended to.   He remained as Drake's guest for a week,
and sent in a report of what he observed to the Spanish
Government.   One at least of Drake's party spoke excellent
Spanish.   This person took San Juan over the ship.   She
showed signs, San Juan said, of rough service, but was
85 still in fine condition, with ample arms, spare ropes,
mattocks, carpenter's tools of all descriptions.   There
were eighty-five men on board all told, fifty of them men-
of-war, the rest young fellows, ship-boys and the like.
Drake himself was treated with great reverence; a sentinel
90 stood always at his cabin door.   He dined alone with
music.

JAMES ANTHONY FROUDE[1]

QUESTIONS

1. Give a title to this extract.
2. Give titles to the paragraphs.

[1]Reprinted from *A History of England* by permission of Longmans, Green
& Co. Ltd., London.

3. Is there any connection in thought between the sentence "At Lima, alas! they were just too late," and the next sentence?

4. Why is the word "hulks" (l. 8) preferable to "ships" in this context?

5. Study the passage "A sail was seen . . . left the shell" (ll. 22–27). Make a note about the length of the sentences in this passage.

6. What would be the loss in effect if the words "At length" (l. 48) were omitted?

7. "They took the kernel. They left the shell." Can you find other examples in this extract of two consecutive sentences in which ideas are sharply contrasted?

8. What had Aladdin's garden got to do with the *Cacafuego*?

9. Give in thirty words the gist of the passage "At Lima, alas! . . . rubies" (ll. 7–16).

10. What sentence links the second paragraph with the first?

11. Divide the second paragraph into four sections; and show how the last sentence of each section comes as a climax. Give a short title (the shorter the better) to each section.

12. "*The full value* was never acknowledged." What other phrases in this paragraph carry the same idea as is conveyed by the italicized words?

13. Explain what is meant by putting a ship's head into the wind, and show that you understand the purpose of Drake's order.

14. "The full value was never acknowledged." The rest of the paragraph is an amplification of this idea. Quote two other examples from this extract of sentences expressing ideas which are subsequently elaborated.

15. Why is the phrase "from off the snows of the Andes" (l. 49) better than "from off the Andes"?

16. What would have been the effect of substituting commas for the semi-colons in l. 61?

17. What is the exact meaning of "all told" (l. 87)? Write a short sentence containing the verb "to tell" in the same sense.

18. Why is San Juan de Anton introduced into the last paragraph? Outsider

19. Which do you consider the most pictorial passage in this extract?

20. Compare the first sentence of the extract with the last and write down any thoughts suggested by the comparison.

21. What is the difference between "ballast" and "cargo"; "bullion" and "coins"?

22. Give the derivation and meaning (in this extract) of—reals, roads, rover, freighted, corsair, character, haul, hailed, plunder.

23. Learn by heart the passage "The *Pelican* sailed two feet . . . the *Pelican's* bows" (ll. 43–53).

24. Write a short paragraph of seven sentences describing Drake from the point of view of one of his ship-boys. The first sentence of the paragraph is, "I always felt ill at ease in his presence." The central ideas of the other six sentences are — his eyes, his aloofness, his iron discipline, his sense of religion, his resourcefulness, the feelings of the crew towards him.

No. III

1. "This, perhaps, may suit," observed the dealer: and then, as he began to re-arise, Markheim bounded from behind upon his victim. The long, skewer-like dagger flashed and fell. The dealer struggled like a hen, striking
5 his temple on the shelf, and then tumbled on the floor in a heap.

2. Time had some score of small voices in that shop, some stately and slow as was becoming to their great age; others garrulous and hurried. All these told out the
10 seconds in an intricate chorus of tickings. Then the passage of a lad's feet, heavily running on the pavement, broke in upon these smaller voices and startled Markheim into the consciousness of his surroundings. He looked

about him awfully.   The candle stood on the counter, its
flame solemnly wagging in a draught; and by that in- 15
considerable movement, the whole room was filled with
noiseless bustle and kept heaving like a sea: the tall
shadows nodding, the gross blots of darkness swelling and
dwindling as with respiration, the faces of the portraits and
the china gods changing and wavering like images in water. 20
The inner door stood ajar, and peered into that leaguer of
shadows with a long slit of daylight like a pointing finger.

3. From these fear-stricken rovings, Markheim's eyes
returned to the body of his victim, where it lay both
humped and sprawling, incredibly small and strangely 25
meaner than in life.   In these poor, miserly clothes, in that
ungainly attitude, the dealer lay like so much sawdust.
Markheim had feared to see it, and, lo! it was nothing.
And yet, as he gazed, this bundle of old clothes and pool of
blood began to find eloquent voices.   There it must lie; 30
there was none to work the cunning hinges or direct the
miracle of locomotion—there it must lie till it was found.
Found! aye, and then?   Then would this dead flesh lift
up a cry that would ring over England, and fill the world
with the echoes of pursuit.   Aye, dead or not, this was still 35
the enemy.   "Time was that when the brains were out . . ."
he thought; and the first word struck into his mind.
Time, now that the deed was accomplished—time, which
had closed for the victim, had become instant and momentous for the slayer.   40

4. The thought was yet in his mind, when, first one and
then another, with every variety of pace and voice—
one deep as the bell from a cathedral turret, another ringing
on its treble notes the prelude of a waltz—the clocks began
to strike the hour of three in the afternoon.   45

5. The sudden outbreak of so many tongues in that
dumb chamber staggered him.   He began to bestir himself,

poignant = piercing

going to and fro with the candle, beleaguered by moving shadows, and startled to the soul by chance reflections. 50 In many rich mirrors, some of home design, some from Venice or Amsterdam, he saw his face repeated and repeated, as it were an army of spies; his own eyes met and detected him; and the sound of his own steps, lightly as they fell, vexed the surrounding quiet. And still, 55 as he continued to fill his pockets, his mind accused him with a sickening iteration, of the thousand faults of his design. He should have chosen a more quiet hour; he should have prepared an alibi; he should not have used a knife; he should have been more cautious, and only 60 bound and gagged the dealer, and not killed him; he should have been more bold, and killed the servant also; he should have done all things otherwise; poignant regrets, weary, incessant toiling of the mind to change what was unchangeable, to plan what was now useless, to be the 65 architect of the irrevocable past. Meanwhile, and behind all this activity, brute terrors, like the scurrying of rats in a deserted attic, filled the more remote chambers of his brain with riot; the hand of the constable would fall heavy on his shoulder, and his nerves would jerk like a 70 hooked fish; or he beheld, in galloping defile, the dock, the prison, the gallows, and the black coffin.

ROBERT LOUIS STEVENSON[1]

QUESTIONS

✓ = omit

because one on surrounding on other book

1. Give a title to this extract.
2. Give titles to the paragraphs.
3. Compare the second and third paragraphs and explain why they are two paragraphs, not one.
4. Show how the second, third, fourth, and fifth paragraphs are linked up. by time

[1]Reprinted from "Markheim" by permission of the publishers, Charles Scribner's Sons.

[handwritten at top: sort of like Edgar Allan Poe but this is more precise — tell tell heart. is more emotional]

5. Can you suggest any reason for the absence of a link between the first and second paragraphs? *[handwritten: cuz a long time has elapsed]*

6. Reduce the second paragraph to a series of brief notes, thus—*Time's voices—chorus of tickings*, etc.

7. (a) Comment upon the position in the paragraph of the sentence, "He looked about him awfully" (l. 13). *[handwritten: introduces m's consciousness to surroun]*
   (b) It divides the paragraph into two sections; what is the difference between the two sections? *[handwritten: hearing and seeing]*

8. Comment upon the word "solemnly" (l. 15).

9. Why is "peered" (l. 21) better than "looked"?

10. What were the "eloquent voices" (l. 30)? *[handwritten: m's thoughts?]*

11. Why does Stevenson, in the third paragraph, dwell upon the meanness of the body?

12. Quote a sentence from this third paragraph which might suggest an answer to No. 11, and underline the significant phrase.

13. Why are "instant" and "momentous" such excellent words in the last sentence of the third paragraph? *[handwritten: because they allow no time for thought]*

14. (a) "Time was that when . . ." (l. 36)? Express the thought of these four words according to modern English usage.
    (b) Complete the sentence "Time was . . ." in such a way as to show his train of thought.
    (c) This is a misquotation from a well-known play of Shakespeare. Can you place it and correct it?

15. Give the gist of the fourth paragraph in fifteen words.

16. Show that "a thousand faults of his design" and "brute terrors" are key-phrases of the last paragraph.

17. Find sentences in which the sounds strikingly help to convey the sense.

18. Find and comment upon four striking similes in this extract.

19. Give the derivation and meaning (in this extract) of garrulous, gross, respiration, leaguer, iteration, poignant, irrevocable, alibi, ajar. (What has "ajar" got to do with "charwoman"?) *[handwritten: in state of discord]*

20. Learn by heart the second and fourth paragraphs.

21. "When I first knew it the house stood at the north end of Pont Street, on the right hand side as you approached the Baptist Chapel. It seemed as though all ages and all countries had been ransacked to furnish this little black-timbered shop."

These are the first two sentences of a description of an old antique-shop. Complete the paragraph by adding several sentences dealing with the contents of the shop. In order to do this consider carefully the words "all ages and all countries."

No. IV

1. In the center of the great city of London lies a small neighborhood, consisting of a cluster of narrow streets and courts, of very venerable and debilitated houses, which goes by the name of Little Britain. Christ Church
5 School and St. Bartholomew's Hospital bound it on the west; Smithfield and Long Lane on the north; Aldersgate Street, like an arm of the sea, divides it from the eastern part of the city; whilst the yawning gulf of Bull-and-Mouth Street separates it from Butcher Lane, and the
10 regions of Newgate. Over this little territory, thus bounded and designated, the great dome of St. Paul's, swelling above the intervening houses of Paternoster Row, Amen Corner, and Ave Maria Lane, looks down with an air of motherly protection.

15 2. This quarter derives its appellation from having been, in ancient times, the residence of the Dukes of Brittany. As London increased, however, rank and fashion rolled off to the west, and trade, creeping on at their heels, took possession of their deserted abodes.
20 For some time Little Britain became the great mart of learning, and was peopled by the busy and prolific race of booksellers: these also gradually deserted it, and, emigrating beyond the great strait of Newgate Street, settled down in Paternoster Row and St. Paul's Church-
25 yard, where they continue to increase and multiply even at the present day.

3. But though thus fallen into decline, Little Britain still bears traces of its former splendor. There are several houses ready to tumble down, the fronts of which are magnificently enriched with old oaken carvings of 30 hideous faces, unknown birds, beasts, and fishes; and fruits and flowers which it would perplex a naturalist to classify. There are also, in Aldersgate Street, certain remains of what were once spacious and lordly family mansions, but which have in latter days been subdivided 35 into several tenements. Here may often be found the family of a petty tradesman, with its trumpery furniture, burrowing among the relics of antiquated finery, in great rumbling time-stained apartments, with fretted ceilings, gilded cornices, and enormous marble fireplaces. The 40 lanes and courts also contain many smaller houses, not on so grand a scale, but, like your small ancient gentry, sturdily maintaining their claims to equal antiquity. These have their gable-ends to the street; great bow windows with diamond panes set in lead, grotesque carvings, 45 and low-arched doorways.

4. In this most venerable and sheltered little nest have I passed several quiet years of existence, comfortably lodged in the second floor of one of the smallest but oldest edifices. My sitting-room is an old wainscoted chamber, 50 with small panels, and set off with a miscellaneous array of furniture. I have a particular respect for three or four high-backed claw-footed chairs, covered with tarnished brocade, which bear the marks of having seen better days, and have doubtless figured in some of the old palaces of 55 Little Britain. They seem to me to keep together, and to look down with sovereign contempt upon their leathern-bottomed neighbors; as I have seen decayed gentry carry a high head among the plebeian society with which they were reduced to associate. The whole front of my 60 sitting-room is taken up with a bow window; on the panes of which are recorded the names of previous occupants

for many generations, mingled with scraps of very indifferent gentleman-like poetry, written in characters which
65 I can scarcely decipher, and which extol the charms of
many a beauty of Little Britain, who has long, long since
bloomed, faded, and passed away. As I am an idle per-
sonage, with no apparent occupation, and pay my bill
regularly every week, I am looked upon as the only inde-
70 pendent gentleman of the neighborhood; and being
curious to learn the internal state of a community so
apparently shut up within itself, I have managed to work
my way into all the concerns and secrets of the place.

5. Little Britain may truly be called the heart's core of
75 the city; the stronghold of true John Bullism. It is a
fragment of London as it was in its better days, with its
antiquated folks and fashions. Here flourish in great
preservation many of the holiday games and customs of
yore. The inhabitants most religiously eat pancakes on
80 Shrove Tuesday, hot cross buns on Good Friday, and roast
goose at Michaelmas; they send love-letters on Valentine's
Day, burn the Pope on the fifth of November, and kiss all
the girls under the mistletoe at Christmas. Roast beef
and plum pudding are also held in superstitious veneration,
85 and port and sherry maintain their grounds as the only
true English wines; all others being considered vile out-
landish beverages.

6. Little Britain has its long catalogue of city wonders,
which its inhabitants consider the wonders of the world;
90 such as the great bell of St. Paul's, which sours all the beer
when it tolls; the figures that strike the hours at St.
Dunstan's clock; the Monument; the lions in the Tower;
and the wooden giants in Guildhall. They still believe in
dreams and fortune-telling, and an old woman that lives
95 in Bull-and-Mouth Street makes a tolerable subsistence by
detecting stolen goods, and promising the girls good
husbands. They are apt to be rendered uncomfortable

by comets and eclipses; and if a dog howls dolefully at night, it is looked upon as a sure sign of a death in the place. There are even many ghost-stories current, partic- 100 ularly concerning the old mansion-houses; in several of which it is said strange sights are sometimes seen. Lords and ladies, the former in full-bottomed wigs, hanging sleeves and swords, the latter in lappets, stays, hoops, and brocade, have been seen walking up and down the great 105 waste chambers, on moonlight nights; and are supposed to be the shades of the ancient proprietors in their court-dresses.

7. Little Britain has likewise its sages and great men. One of the most important of the former is a tall, dry 110 old gentleman, of the name of Skryme, who keeps a small apothecary's shop. He has a cadaverous countenance, full of cavities and projections; with a brown circle round each eye, like a pair of horn spectacles. He is much thought of by the old women, who consider him as a kind 115 of conjurer, because he has two or three stuffed alligators hanging up in his shop, and several snakes in bottles. He is a great reader of almanacs and newspapers, and is much given to pore over alarming accounts of plots, conspiracies, fires, earthquakes, and volcanic eruptions; 120 which last phenomena he considers as signs of the times. He has always some dismal tale of the kind to deal out to his customers with their doses; and thus at the same time puts both soul and body into an uproar. He is a great believer in omens and predictions; and has the prophecies 125 of Robert Nixon and Mother Shipton by heart. No man can make so much out of an eclipse, or even an unusually dark day; and he shook the tail of the last comet over the heads of his customers and disciples until they were nearly frightened out of their wits. He has lately got hold 130 of a popular legend or prophecy, on which he has been unusually eloquent. There has been a saying current among the ancient sybils, who treasure up these things,

that when the grasshopper on the top of the Exchange
135 shook hands with the dragon on the top of Bow Church
steeple, fearful events would take place.   This strange
conjunction, it seems, has as strangely come to pass.   The
same architect has been engaged lately on the repairs of
the cupola of the Exchange, and the steeple of Bow Church;
140 and, fearful to relate, the dragon and the grasshopper
actually lie, cheek by jowl, in the yard of his workshop.

8. "Others," as Mr. Skryme is accustomed to say,
"may go star-gazing, and look for conjunctions in the
heavens, but here is a conjunction on the earth, near at
145 home, and under our own eyes, which surpasses all the
signs and calculations of astrologers."   Since these por-
tentous weathercocks have thus laid their heads together,
wonderful events had already occurred. The good old
king, notwithstanding that he had lived eighty-two years,
150 had all at once given up the ghost; another king had
mounted the throne; a royal duke had died suddenly—
another in France had been murdered; there had been
Radical meetings in all parts of the Kingdom; the bloody
scenes at Manchester; the great plot in Cato Street;—
155 and, above all, the Queen had returned to England!
All these sinister events are recounted by Mr. Skryme
with a mysterious look and a dismal shake of the head;
and being taken with his drugs and associated in the minds
of his auditors with stuffed sea-monsters, bottled serpents,
160 and his own visage, which is a title-page of tribulation,
they have spread great gloom through the minds of the
people of Little Britain.   They shake their heads whenever
they go by Bow Church, and observe, that they never
expected any good to come of taking down that steeple,
165 which in old times told nothing but glad tidings, as the
history of Whittington and his Cat bears witness.

9. The rival oracle of Little Britain is a substantial
cheesemonger, who lives in a fragment of one of the old

family mansions, and is as magnificently lodged as a
round-bellied mite in the midst of one of his own Cheshires. 170
Indeed, he is a man of no little standing and importance;
and his renown extends through Huggin Lane, and Lad
Lane, and even unto Aldermanbury. His opinion is very
much taken in affairs of state, having read the Sunday
papers for the last half century, together with the *Gentle-* 175
man's Magazine, Rapin's *History of England*, and the
Naval Chronicle. His head is stored with invaluable
maxims which have borne the test of time and use for
centuries. It is his firm opinion that "it is a moral impossible," so long as England is true to herself, that any- 180
thing can shake her; and he has much to say on the
subject of the national debt; which, somehow or other,
he proves to be a great national bulwark and blessing.
He passed the greater part of his life in the purlieus of
Little Britain, until of late years, when, having become 185
rich, and grown into the dignity of a Sunday cane, he
begins to take his pleasure and see the world. He has
therefore made several excursions to Hampstead, Highgate,
and other neighboring towns, where he has passed whole
afternoons in looking back upon the metropolis through a 190
telescope, and endeavoring to descry the steeple of St.
Bartholomew's. Not a stage-coachman of Bull-and-
Mouth Street but touches his hat as he passes; and he is
considered quite a patron at the coach-office of the Goose
and Gridiron, St. Paul's Churchyard. His family have 195
been very urgent for him to make an expedition to Margate,
but he has great doubts of those new gimcracks, the steam-
boats, and, indeed, thinks himself too advanced in life
to undertake sea voyages.

10. Little Britain has occasionally its factions and 200
divisions, and party spirit ran very high at one time in
consequence of two rival "Burial Societies" being set up
in the place. One held its meeting at the Swan and Horse
Shoe, and was patronized by the cheesemonger; the other

205 at the Cock and Crown, under the auspices of the apothecary; it is needless to say that the latter was the most
flourishing. I have passed an evening or two at each,
and have acquired much valuable information, as to the
best mode of being buried, the comparative merits of
210 churchyards, together with divers hints on the subject of
patent-iron coffins. I have heard the question discussed
in all its bearings as to the legality of prohibiting the latter
on account of their durability. The feuds occasioned by
these societies have happily died of late; but they were
215 for a long time prevailing themes of controversy, the
people of Little Britain being extremely solicitous of
funeral honors and of lying comfortably in their
graves.

11. Besides these two funeral societies, there is a third
220 of quite a different cast, which tends to throw the sunshine
of good humor over the whole neighborhood. It meets
once a week at a little old-fashioned house, kept by a
jolly publican of the name of Wagstaff, and bearing for
insignia a resplendent half-moon, with a most seductive
225 bunch of grapes. The whole edifice is covered with
inscriptions to catch the eye of the thirsty wayfarer;
such as "Truman, Hanbury & Co's Entire," "Wine,
Rum, and Brandy Vaults," "Old Tom, Rum, and Com-
pounds," etc. This, indeed, has been a temple of Bacchus
230 and Momus from time immemorial. It has always been
in the family of the Wagstaffs, so that its history is
tolerably preserved by the present landlord. It was much
frequented by the gallants and cavalieros of the reign of
Elizabeth, and was looked into now and then by the wits
235 of Charles the Second's day. But what Wagstaff princi-
pally prides himself upon is, that Henry the Eighth, in
one of his nocturnal rambles, broke the head of one of
his ancestors with his famous walking-staff. This, however, is considered as rather a dubious and vain-glorious
240 boast of the landlord.

12. The club, which now holds its weekly sessions here, goes by the name of "the Roaring Lads of Little Britain." They abound in old catches, glees, and choice stories, that are traditional in the place, and not to be met with in any other part of the metropolis. There is a mad-cap 245 undertaker who is inimitable at a merry song; but the life of the club, and indeed the prime wit of Little Britain, is bully Wagstaff himself. His ancestors were all wags before him, and he has inherited with the inn a large stock of songs and jokes, which go with it from generation to 250 generation as heirlooms. He is a dapper little fellow, with bandy legs and pot belly, a red face, with a moist merry eye, and a little shock of gray hair behind. At the opening of every club-night he is called in to sing his "Confession of Faith," which is the famous old drinking trowl from 255 *Gammer Gurton's Needle.* He sings it, to be sure, with many variations, as he received it from his father's lips; for it has been a standing favorite at the Half-Moon and Bunch of Grapes ever since it was written; nay, he affirms that his predecessors have often had the honor of singing 260 it before the nobility and gentry at Christmas mummeries, when Little Britain was in all its glory.

13. It would do one's heart good to hear, on a club night, the shouts of merriment, the snatches of song, and now and then the choral bursts of half a dozen discordant 265 voices, which issue from this jovial mansion. At such times the street is lined with listeners, who enjoy a delight equal to that of gazing into a confectioner's window, or snuffing up the steams of a cook-shop.

14. There are two annual events which produce great 270 stir and sensation in Little Britain; these are St. Bartholomew's fair, and the Lord Mayor's day. During the time of the fair, which is held in the adjoining regions of Smithfield, there is nothing going on but gossiping and gadding about. The late quiet streets of Little Britain are 275

overrun with an irruption of strange figures and faces;
every tavern is a scene of rout and revel.   The fiddle and
the song are heard from the tap-room, morning, noon, and
night; and at each window may be seen some group of
280 boon companions, with half-shut eyes, hats on one side,
pipe in mouth, and tankard in hand, fondling and prosing,
and singing maudlin songs over their liquor.   Even the
sober decorum of private families, which I must say is
rigidly kept up at other times among my neighbors,
285 is no proof against this Saturnalia.   There is no such
thing as keeping maid-servants within doors.   Their
brains are absolutely set maddening with Punch and the
Puppet Show; the Flying Horses; Signior Polito; the
Fire-Eater; the celebrated Mr. Paap; and the Irish
290 Giant.   The children, too, lavish all their holiday money
in toys and gilt gingerbread, and fill the house with
the Lilliputian din of drums, trumpets, and penny
whistles. *very small allusion to Gulliver's Travel*

15. But the Lord Mayor's day is the great anniversary.
295 The Lord Mayor is looked up to by the inhabitants of
Little Britain as the grandest potentate upon earth; his
gilt coach with six horses as the summit of human splendor; and his procession, with all the Sheriffs and
Aldermen in his train, as the greatest of earthly pageants.
300 How they exult in the idea, that the King himself dare
not enter the city, without first knocking at the gate of
Temple Bar, and asking permission of the Lord Mayor;
for if he did, heaven and earth! there is no knowing what
might be the consequence.   The man in armor who rides
305 before the Lord Mayor, and is the city champion, has orders
to cut down everybody that offends against the dignity of
the city; and then there is the little man with a velvet
porringer on his head, who sits at the window of the state
coach, and holds the city sword, as long as a pike-staff—
310 Odd's blood!   If he once draws that sword, Majesty itself
is not safe!

16. Under the protection of this mighty potentate, therefore, the good people of Little Britain sleep in peace. Temple Bar is an effectual barrier against all interior foes; and as to foreign invasion, the Lord Mayor has but to 315 throw himself into the Tower, call in the train bands, and put the standing army of beef-eaters under arms, and he may bid defiance to the world!

fungus – lives on something else

17. Thus wrapped up in its own concerns, its own habits, and its own opinions, Little Britain has long flourished as 320 a sound heart to this great fungus metropolis. I have pleased myself with considering it as a chosen spot, where the principles of sturdy John Bullism were garnered up, like seed corn, to renew the national character, when it had run to waste and degeneracy. I have rejoiced also in 325 the general spirit of harmony that prevailed throughout it; for though there might now and then be a few clashes of opinion between the adherents of the cheesemonger and the apothecary, and an occasional feud between the burial societies, yet these were but transient clouds, and 330 soon passed away. The neighbors met with goodwill, parted with a shake of the hand, and never abused each other except behind their backs.

WASHINGTON IRVING

✓ omit

QUESTIONS

1. Give a title to this extract.   *provincial*   *Sheltered Little Britain*
✓2. Give titles to the paragraphs.
3. Find a sentence in this extract which summarizes the central idea of the extract. *line 319*
4. Find a phrase in the first paragraph which indicates the scope of the paragraph. *line 11*
5. Comment on the suitability of the words "rolled," "creeping," and "emigrating" (second paragraph). Why, for example, is "moving" not so good as "emigrating"?

6. What words or phrases in the third paragraph repeat the idea of splendor?

7. What is the relation of the first sentence of the third paragraph to the paragraph as a whole?

8. The central ideas of the third paragraph are splendor and decay . . . ? Supply one word for the blank.

9. Why is "burrowing" such an excellent word in l. 38? ——

10. Divide the fourth paragraph into two sections:
    (a) The writer's . . apartment
    (b) The writer's . position in So
    Supply one word for each blank and show where you would divide the paragraph.

11. What are the two key-phrases of the fourth paragraph?

12. (a) Write down all the words and phrases in the fourth paragraph that remind us of the antiquity of place.
    (b) Why cannot the fourth and fifth paragraphs be transposed without impairing the sequence of thought?

13. What is the phrase in the fifth paragraph of which the rest of the paragraph is an elaboration?

14. The sentence "Here flourish . . . yore" (l. 77) repeats the idea of the preceding sentence. What is it? Where else in the paragraph is the same idea indicated?

15. In what way would the sequence of thought be spoiled, if the sentence about the howling dog were transposed to the end of the paragraph?

16. Give two phrases from the sixth paragraph which indicate general ideas subsequently elaborated in the paragraph.

17. The word "superstitions" will not cover the whole of the sixth paragraph. What part will it not cover? Can you suggest one word that will cover the whole paragraph?

18. The two sages mentioned are the apothecary and the cheesemonger. Consider the context carefully and explain why it was better to introduce us to the apothecary first.

19. Omitting the first sentence of the seventh paragraph we may analyze the thought of the passage as far as "by heart" (l. 126) as follows:
    (a) "One . . . spectacles." Skryme's . . . and . . .

(b) "He is much thought of . . . bottles": his . . . *reputation*

(c) "He is a great reader . . . uproar": his . . . *effect, influence*

(d) "He is a great believer . . . heart": his . . . *prophecies*

Supply one word for each of the blanks.

20. Show that the words "and body" add to the humor of the passage (l. 124).

21. How did he "shake the tail of the last comet, etc."? Here you must explain by getting rid of the metaphor.

22. What is the relation of the eighth to the seventh paragraph?

23. What are "conjunctions in the heavens" (l. 143)?

24. Compare the first and last sentences of the eighth paragraph.

25. What is the difference between an astrologer and an astronomer?

26. Look up the derivation of the word "mysterious" (l. 157) and comment on the suitability of the word here.

27. What is the significance of the phrase "a title-page of tribulation" (l. 160)? (You must consider what a title-page is, and for what purpose we have it.)

28. What feature in common have all the incidents related in the passage "The good old king . . . to England!"?

29. In what respects is the information given about the cheesemonger *(a)* fuller *(b)* slighter than that given about the apothecary? In handling this question you should organize your answer under various headings—e.g. physical characteristics, etc.

30. How does the sentence "Not a stage-coachman . . . St. Paul's Churchyard" arise from the preceding sentence?

31. "The cheesemonger's attitude with reference to the Margate expedition illustrates his . . . outlook on life." Supply one word for the blank.

32. Explain the joke in the sentence "it is needless to say that the latter was the most flourishing" (l. 206). What is innuendo? Note the derivation of the word.

33. Who were Bacchus and Momus (l. 229)? *god of ridicule.* Rewrite the sentence, getting rid of the allusions to Bacchus and Momus yet giving Irving's full meaning.

34. What sentence in the eleventh paragraph justifies the qualification "tolerably" in l. 232?

innuendo - you allude to someone in a derogatory fashion.

things don't go well together

35. What is "incongruity"? Illustrate it by quoting and commenting on one sentence from the twelfth paragraph.

36. What is the exact significance of "catches," "glees," "bully" "trowl," "mummeries"?

37. What traits in Wagstaff's character are indicated,
  (a) Exclusively in the eleventh paragraph,
  (b) Exclusively in the twelfth paragraph,
  (c) In both paragraphs?
  You should use single nouns or short noun-phrases to indicate these traits and refer to those parts of the paragraphs where you find them.

38. What is the point of the comparison "equal to that, etc." (l. 268)?

39. What were the "strange figures and faces" (l. 276)?

40. What is the key-sentence of the fourteenth paragraph?

41. Divide the fourteenth paragraph into three sections and supply a short phrase to indicate the scope of each section.

42. What is Saturnalia? If you don't know, before looking it up, study the context again and have a guess at it.

time of great unconfined revelry

43. Give in not more than twelve words the gist of the passage "There is no such thing . . . Giant" (l. 285).

44. What is the key-sentence of the fifteenth paragraph?

45. What is there in the fifteenth paragraph to suggest the leading idea of the sixteenth paragraph?

46. What is the relation of the last paragraph to the extract as a whole?

47. Why is the metropolis called "fungus" (l. 321)?

48. Why is "garnered" (l. 323) better than "gathered"? Name two other words connected etymologically with "garnered."

49. If we take "a sound heart to this great fungus metropolis" as the key-phrase of the last paragraph, why is it appropriate to speak in the same paragraph of "the general spirit of harmony"?

50. What is a Parthian shaft? Illustrate your answer from the last paragraph of the extract.

51. Give the derivation and meaning (in this extract) of the following words—trumpery, fretted, grotesque, outlandishly, current, cadaverous, dismal, cupola, prevailing, auspices, abound, train-bands, dapper.

fresco (Ital.)
painting on
question
hall
frieze - carving
little & active
spruce & trim

52. Learn by heart the fifth paragraph.
53. "It was the sleepiest village I had ever entered." This is
    the first sentence of a paragraph describing a village.
    Complete the paragraph, developing and emphasizing
    the word "sleepiest." Develop the same idea with
    reference to the inhabitants in a second paragraph of
    which the following is the beginning: "The inhabitants,
    too, might have been born in their sleep."

*level of language
is simple, everyday,
not allusive or
literary or consultative*

No. V

1. At first when you see the coolie on the road, bearing
his load, it is as a pleasing object that he strikes the eye. *a)*
In his blue rags, a blue of all colors from indigo to tur-
quoise and then to the paleness of a milky sky, he fits the
landscape. He seems exactly right as he trudges along 5
the narrow causeway between the rice-fields or climbs
a green hill. His clothing consists of no more than a short
coat and a pair of trousers; and if he had a suit which was
at the beginning all of a piece, he never thinks when it
comes to patching to choose a bit of stuff of the same 10
color. He takes anything that comes handy. From sun
and rain he protects his head with a straw hat shaped like
an extinguisher with a preposterously wide, flat brim.

2. You see a string of coolies come along, one after the
other, each with a pole on his shoulders from the ends of 15
which hang two great bales, and they make an agreeable *c)*
pattern. It is amusing to watch their hurrying reflections *b)*
in the padi water. You watch their faces as they pass you.
They are good-natured faces and frank, you would have
said, if it had not been drilled into you that the oriental 20
is inscrutable; and when you see them lying down with
their loads under a banyan tree by a wayside shrine,
smoking and chatting gaily, if you have tried to lift the

bales they carry for thirty miles or more a day, it seems
25 natural to feel admiration for their endurance and their
spirit.   But you will be thought somewhat absurd if you
mention your admiration to the old residents of China.
You will be told with a tolerant shrug of the shoulders
that the coolies are animals, and for two thousand years
30 from father to son have carried burdens, so it is no wonder
if they do it cheerfully.   And indeed you can see for your-
self that they begin early, for you will encounter little
children with a yoke on their shoulders staggering under
the weight of vegetable baskets.

35   3. The day wears on and it grows warmer. The coolies
take off their coats and walk stripped to the waist.   Then
sometimes in a man resting for an instant, his load on the
ground but the pole still on his shoulders so that he has to
rest slightly crouched, you see the poor, tired heart beating
40 against the ribs: you see it as plainly as in some cases of
heart disease in the out-patients' room of a hospital.
It is strangely distressing to watch.   Then also you see
the coolies' backs.   The pressure of the pole for long years,
day after day, has made hard red scars, and sometimes
45 even there are open sores, great sores without bandages
or dressing that rub against the wood; but the strangest
thing of all is that sometimes, as though nature sought to
adapt man for these cruel uses to which he is put, an odd
malformation seems to have arisen so that there is a sort
50 of hump, like a camel's, against which the pole rests.   But
beating heart or angry sore, bitter rain or burning sun
notwithstanding, they go on eternally, from dawn till dusk,
year in year out, from childhood to the extreme of age.
You see old men without an ounce of fat on their bodies,
55 their skin loose on their bones, wizened, their little faces
wrinkled and ape-like, with hair thin and grey; and they
totter under their burdens to the edge of the grave in
which at last they shall have rest.   And still the coolies
go, not exactly running, but not walking either, sidling

quickly, with their eyes on the ground to choose the spot to 60
place their feet, and on their faces a strained, anxious
expression.   You can make no longer a pattern of them as
they wend their way.   Their effort oppresses you.   You
are filled with a useless compassion.

4. In China it is man that is the beast of burden.   65

5. "To be harassed by the wear and tear of life, and to
pass rapidly through it without the possibility of arresting
one's course—is not this pitiful indeed?   To labor
without ceasing, and then, without living to enjoy the
fruit, worn out, to depart, suddenly, one knows not 70
whither—is not that a just cause for grief?"

6. So wrote the Chinese mystic.

W. SOMERSET MAUGHAM[1]

QUESTIONS

1. Give a title to the essay.
2. Give titles to the first three paragraphs.
3. What single sentence in the essay best indicates the idea
    of the essay?
4. What, for the purposes of the first paragraph, is the signifi-
    cant feature of the coolie's clothing?
5. Having regard to the essay as a whole, what do you think
    is the most significant phrase in the first paragraph?
6. Why can you not transpose the first two paragraphs without
    impairing the structure of the essay?
7. (a) What is the climax of the essay?
    (b) What single statement in the second paragraph points
        to the climax?
8. With what is the word "lift" (l. 23) contrasted?
9. "The experienced resident in China knows that it is ...."

[1]Reprinted from *On a Chinese Screen*, copyright, 1922, by Doubleday, Doran
& Co., Inc.

good nature

not . . . , that makes the coolie bear his burden cheerfully." Supply one word for each blank.

10. From the third paragraph choose three short sentences *a*, *b*, *c*, and after them write three sharply contrasting sentences *a*, *b*, *c*, taken from the first two paragraphs.

11. Divide the third paragraph into four sections showing where each section begins and ends. The sections may be indicated thus:

    (*a*) The . . . of the coolies.
    (*b*) The . . . of their backs.
    (*c*) The . . . of their . . .
    (*d*) The . . . of the beholder.

Supply one word for each blank.

12. "They totter under their burdens . . . rest" (l. 56). What other sentence in the essay does this recall? (The word "totter" may help you.)

13. "In which at last they shall have rest" (l. 58). How does this add to the effect of the passage?

14. What is the connection in thought between the last two sentences of the third paragraph and the one immediately preceding?

15. Why is your compassion "useless"?

16. Summarize in fifteen words the passage "But beating heart . . . anxious expression" (ll. 50–62).

17. What other word in the essay is connected in derivation with the Latin word that gives us "strained" (l. 61)?

18. Write down the names of five or six emotions which this essay suggests.

19. Give the derivation and meaning (in this essay) of—causeway, inscrutable, shrine, distressing, sidling, compassion, mystic.

20. Learn by heart the passage "But beating heart . . . anxious expression."

21. Complete the paragraph of which the following is the first sentence: "Under a blazing July sun the gypsy caravan crawled wearily through the countryside." Your aim is to call up a vivid picture of the caravan.

No. VI

1. I take it that in the lower animals misery can result from two causes only—restraint and disease: consequently, that animals in a state of nature are not miserable. They are not hindered nor held back. Whether the animal is migrating, or burying himself in his hibernating nest or den; or flying from some rapacious enemy, which he may or may not be able to escape; or feeding, or sleeping, or fighting, or courting, or incubating, however many days or weeks this process may last—in all things he is obeying the impulse that is strongest in him at the time—he is doing what he wants to do, the one thing that makes him happy.

2. As to disease, it is so rare in wild animals, or in a large majority of cases so quickly proves fatal, that, compared with what we call disease in our own species, it is practically non-existent. "The struggle for existence," in so far as animals in a state of nature are concerned, is a metaphorical struggle; and the strife, short and sharp, which is so common in nature, is not misery, although it results in pain, since it is pain that kills or is soon outlived. Fear there is, just as in fine weather there are clouds in the sky; and just as the shadow of the cloud passes, so does fear pass from the wild creature when the object that excited it has vanished from sight. And when death comes, it comes unexpectedly, and is not the death that we know, even before we taste of it, thinking of it with apprehension all our lives long, but a sudden blow that takes away consciousness—the touch of something that numbs the nerves—merely the prick of a needle. In whatever way the animal perishes, whether by violence, or excessive cold, or decay, his death is a comparatively easy one. So long as he is fighting with or struggling to escape from an enemy, wounds are not felt as wounds,

and scarcely hurt him—as we know from our own experi-
35 ence; and when overcome, if death be not practically
instantaneous, as in the case of a small bird seized by a cat,
the disabling grip or blow is itself a kind of anodyne,
producing insensibility to pain. This, too, is a matter of
human experience. To say nothing of those who fall in
40 battle, men have often been struck down and fearfully
lacerated by lions, tigers, jaguars, and other savage beasts;
and, after having been rescued by their companions, have
recounted this strange thing. Even when there was no
loss of consciousness, when they saw and knew that the
45 animal was rending their flesh, they seemed not to feel it,
and were, at the time, indifferent to the fate that had
overtaken them.

3. It is the same in death from cold. The strong,
well-nourished man, overtaken by a snowstorm on some
50 pathless, uninhabited waste, may experience some ex-
ceedingly bitter moments, or even hours, before he gives
up the struggle. The physical pain is simply nothing;
the whole bitterness is in the thought that he must die.
The horror at the thought of annihilation, the remem-
55 brance of all the happiness he is now about to lose, of dear
friends, of those whose lives will be dimmed with grief
for his loss, of all his cherished dreams of the future—the
sting of all this is so sharp that, compared with it, the
creeping coldness in his blood is nothing more than a
60 slight discomfort, and is scarcely felt. By and by he is
overcome by drowsiness, and ceases to struggle; the
torturing visions fade from his mind, and his only thought
is to lie down and sleep. And when he sleeps he passes
away; very easily, very painlessly, for the pain was of the
65 mind, and was over long before death ensued.

4. The bird, however hard the frost may be, flies briskly
to his customary roosting-place, and, with beak tucked
into his wing, falls asleep. He has no apprehensions;

only the hot blood grows colder and colder, the pulse feebler as he sleeps, and at midnight, or in the early morning, he drops from his perch—dead.

5. Yesterday he lived and moved, responsive to a thousand external influences, reflecting earth and sky in his small brilliant brain as in a looking-glass; also he had a various language, the inherited knowledge of his race, and the faculty of flight, by means of which he could shoot, meteor-like, across the sky, and pass swiftly from place to place; and with it such perfect control over all his organs, such marvelous certitude in all his motions, as to be able to drop himself plumb down from the tallest tree-top or out of the void air, on to a slender spray, and scarcely cause its leaves to tremble. Now, on this morning, he lies stiff and motionless; if you were to take him up and drop him from your hand, he would fall to the ground like a stone or a lump of clay—so easy and swift is the passage from life to death in wild nature! But he was never miserable.

6. Those of my readers who have seen much of animals in a state of nature, will agree that death from decay, or old age, is very rare among them. In that state the fullest vigor, with brightness of all the faculties, is so important that probably in ninety-nine cases in a hundred any falling off in strength, or decay of any sense, results in some fatal accident. Death by misadventure, as we call it, is Nature's ordinance, the end designed for a very large majority of her children. Nevertheless, animals do sometimes live on without accident to the very end of their term, to fade peacefully away at the last. I have myself witnessed such cases in mammals and birds; and one such case, which profoundly impressed me, and is vividly remembered, I will describe. One morning in the late summer, while walking in the fields at my home in South America, I noticed a few purple martins, large, beautiful swallows

common in that region, engaged, at a considerable height,
105 in the aerial exercises in which they pass so much of their
time each day. By and by one of the birds separated
itself from the others, and, circling slowly downward,
finally alighted on the ground not far from me. I walked
on; but the action of the bird had struck me as unusual
110 and strange, and before going far, I turned and walked
back to the spot where it continued sitting on the ground,
quite motionless. It made no movement when I approached to within four yards of it; and after I had stood
still at that distance for a minute or so, attentively regard-
115 ing it, I saw it put out one wing and turn over on its side.
I at once took it up in my hand, and found that it was
already quite dead. It was a large example of its species,
and its size, together with a something of dimness in the
glossy purple color of the upper plumage, seemed to show
120 that it was an old bird. But it was uninjured, and when
I dissected it no trace of disease was discernible. I concluded that it was an old bird that had died solely from
natural failure of the life-energy.

W. H. HUDSON[1]
wrote Green Mansions

QUESTIONS

✓ = omit

1. Give a title to this extract.
2. Give titles to the paragraphs.
3. Why is the phrase "in a state of nature" (l. 3) necessary
   to Hudson's argument?
4. What is the relation of the last fifteen words of the first
   paragraph to the whole paragraph?
5. Express in a single word the predominating idea of the
   passage "They are not hindered . . . happy" (ll. 3-12).
6. What is the key-sentence of the first paragraph?   *lines 3-4*
7. The second paragraph contains a sentence which summarizes the argument of the whole extract. Find the
   sentence.   *24-29*

[1]Reprinted from *Birds in a Village* by permission of J. M. Dent & Sons,
Ltd., London, and E. P. Dutton & Co., Inc., New York.

8. What, for the purpose of Hudson's argument, is the essential difference between "pain" and "misery"?

9. Study the passage "Fear there is . . . sight" (ll. 21–24). Now supply one word for the following blank: "The fear which the wild creature knows is . . ."

10. What is the point of the simile "just as . . . sky" (ll. 21–22)?

11. Supply one word for each of the blanks in the following: "The second paragraph deals with the . . . of the wild animal, the . . . of the wild animal, and the . . . of the wild animal."

12. What is "this strange thing" (l. 43)?

13. Give a phrase of not more than eight words that summarizes the passage "Even when . . . overtaken them" (ll. 43–47).

14. Why does Hudson draw attention to the fact that the man (in the third paragraph) is strong and well-nourished?

15. What are the two key-sentences of the third paragraph?

16. "The effective writer spends his resources in showing what a thing *is*, rather than in showing what it *is not*." Discuss this remark with reference to the third paragraph.

17. Has the phrase "with beak tucked into his wing" (l. 67) anything to do with Hudson's argument? If not, why does he insert it?

18. In what ways is the death of the bird
    (a) similar to
    (b) different from the death of the man (in the third paragraph)?

19. What is climax? How does the question arise from a study of the fourth paragraph?

20. The fifth paragraph falls into two sections.
    (a) What are they?
    (b) What would be the loss to the paragraph as a whole if the first section were omitted?

21. A man is often said to reflect; the man in the snowstorm no doubt did a considerable amount of reflecting. A mirror also reflects. When a mirror reflects, it gives back (if it is a good one) an exact image of what is before it. But when a man reflects . . . ? With this train of thought in mind, comment upon the extraordinary aptness of the simile "as in a looking-glass"

(l. 74), and show why "brain" is a better word in this context than "mind."

22. Explain very carefully the full significance of the similes "like a stone or a lump of clay."

23. In the fifth paragraph there is a five-fold antithesis—that is, there are five ideas in the first section which are brought into contact with five ideas in the second section. Write out in one column the single words, phrases, clauses, or sentences which indicate those ideas, and in a parallel column the single words, etc., which indicate the contrasting ideas.

24. In the sixth paragraph what phrase in the second sentence is brought into contrast with "death from decay, or old age"?

25. Divide the sixth paragraph into three sections.

26. (a) In what way does the sixth paragraph differ from all the other paragraphs?

    (b) Does the paragraph advance Hudson's argument? (Consider whether his argument would be incomplete without this paragraph.)

27. Give the derivation and meaning (in this passage) of—hibernating, rapacious, incubating, anodyne, apprehension, plumb, faculties, ordinance, mammals, species.

28. Learn by heart the fourth paragraph.

29. Write a paragraph of which the opening sentence is "If birds be capable of misery it is only in the unnatural conditions of a caged life." Use antithesis by presenting first a picture of the bird in its natural surroundings; then a picture of it in its present surroundings (sky— trees—greenery—shade—living water—mating—pursuit of food; brick walls—smoke—wire bars—roar of traffic. These are mere suggestions.).

No. VII

1. The Celt remained with diminished luster, but the Roman passed away out of the story of Britain. As has been said above, he left behind him three things as perma-

nent legacies—the traditional site of London, the Roman
roads, and Welsh Christianity.   5

2. It is a moot point whether or not, during the fiercest
time of the Saxon Conquest, London was ever completely
abandoned. If, as is possible, it was at one time quite
deserted, its re-establishment as a Saxon town on a more
modest scale followed very soon, for by the time of Bede 10
(A. D. 700) it was again spoken of as an important center
of commerce, as commerce was accounted in those barbarous times. We may fairly regard the Romans as the
founders of London. The concentration of their road
system at that point in the navigable Thames, made 15
London's commercial revival certain, for the Romans,
when they left England, did not take their roads away with
them.

3. The importance of the Roman roads after their
makers had gone, lay in this: no one made any more hard 20
roads in the island until the turnpike movement of the
Eighteenth Century. Throughout the Dark Ages and in
early medieval times, these stone highways still traversed
an island otherwise relapsed to disunion and barbarism.
The Roman roads greatly increased the speed of the Saxon, 25
Danish and Norman Conquests, and aided, both in peace
and in war, the slow work of Saxon and Norman Kings
in uniting England as one State, and making the English
nation. Thanks to the Roman legacy, Britain had better
national highways under the Saxon heptarchy than in 30
Stuart times, though in the later period there were more
by-roads. The imperial stone causeways, often elevated
some feet above the ground, ran from sea to sea, generally
keeping the higher land, but where needful marching
majestically over bog and through forest. If the bridges 35
soon fell in from neglect, the paved fords remained.
For centuries wild tribes who only knew the name of
Cæsar as a myth, trod his gigantic highways and gave

them the fantastic names of Watling Street, Ermine Street,
40 and the Foss Way. Gradually the stones subsided and
men were too careless and ignorant to replace them.
Next, the road was used as a quarry, when the medieval
Englishman, having somewhat exhausted his timber,
began to build for himself dwelling-houses of stone. From
45 driving roads they declined into pack-horse tracks, finally
disappearing for the most part in moor or plough-land.
Stretches of them have been repaired and modernized,
and the motor car now shoots along the path of the legions.
But other stretches—and those the best beloved—are
50 reserved for the Briton or Saxon who still fares on foot;
they are to be traced as green lanes, starting up out of
nowhere and ending in nothing, going for miles straight
as a die through the magical old English countryside.

4. The third legacy of the Romans was Welsh Chris-
55 tianity. Their latest importation into Britain survived
all their older and more characteristic institutions. There
are but few traces of Christianity in the Romano-British
world revealed by the spade of the archæologist, and this
makes all the more remarkable its survival as the only
30 relic of that civilization among the Welsh. One reason
was this: when the military and political system of the
Cæsars departed from Britain, it never returned; but
missionaries of the Christian religion kept coming back
from the Latinized continent to encourage the Welsh
65 during the dark period after the Northumbrian wall was
broken, when the Picts and Scots were attacking from
north and west, and the Saxons from south and east.
Deserted by the rest of the civilized world, the Welsh were
not forgotten by the missionaries. Such a one was Saint
70 Germanus, the traditional hero of the "Hallelujah victory"
that he won over an army of combined Picts and Saxons
in 430. The story tells how the Saint, formerly a distinguished soldier of Rome in Gaul, having come to Britain
on a mission to put down Pelagian heretics, returned to his

old trade, took command of the multitude of frightened [75] Britons, and led them to victory over the dreaded heathen invader. It may indeed be an exaggerated clerical account of a transaction that is otherwise totally lost to our knowledge, but it is highly characteristic of that period—symbolic even. The Christian clergy, men of affairs and [80] education when such qualities were becoming rare, stood in the gap whence the Roman soldier and governor were in retreat. In the day of trouble the Christian faith got a hold over the Welsh, which had not belonged to it as the official religion of later Roman rule in Britain. We [85] shall see the same process repeated when the Saxons, newly Christianized, in their turn pass under the hammer of the heathen Danes and Norsemen. "Give peace in our time, O Lord, because there is none other that fighteth for us but only Thou, O God," has a curious sound in the [90] modern English liturgy; it seems to speak of the Christian God as the only ally, but not a very formidable safeguard in a world all gone wrong. But to a Welshman, dispossessed by the Saxons in the Fifth Century, or a Saxon dispossessed by the Danes in the Ninth, it would have [95] appeared a very just statement of the case.

GEORGE MACAULAY TREVELYAN[1]

QUESTIONS   omit

1. Give a title to the extract.
2. Give titles to the paragraphs.
3. What relation has the first paragraph to the extract as a whole?
4. Show that the connection in thought between the second and third paragraphs is closer and more obvious than that between the third and the fourth.
5. What is the key-sentence of the second paragraph?
6. What does the clause "as commerce . . . times" (l. 12) contribute to the thought of the sentence?

---

[1]Reprinted from *History of England* by permission of Longmans, Green & Co., Ltd., London.

7. Study the sentence "Throughout the Dark Ages . . . barbarism" (ll. 22–24). Now fill in the blanks in the following: "These stone highways still bore evidence to an island that at one time had been . . . and . . .''

8. What other single words or phrases does Trevelyan use in the third paragraph to indicate Roman roads?

9. Why does Trevelyan use "national" in l. 30, but "imperial' in l. 32?

10. What phrase in the passage "The imperial stone causeways . . . forest" (ll. 32–35) recalls ideas that one naturally associates with "imperial"?

11. If in l. 44 Trevelyan had written "began to build for himself stone dwelling-houses," in what way would the sentence have lost its quality?

12. Divide the third paragraph into three sections.
    - (a) The . . . and . . . of the Roman highways.
    - (b) Their . . .
    - (c) Their . . .

    Fill with single words the blanks above and indicate where the divisions occur by writing out the last two words of each section.

13. What figure of speech is illustrated by the phrase "the spade of the archæologist" (l. 58)? Rewrite the sentence, getting rid of this figure of speech. What effect is produced by using this figure?

14. "One reason was this" (l. 60). Reason for what?

15. The fourth paragraph may be divided as follows:
    - (a) Statement of a result.
    - (b) The cause of this result.
    - (c) Particular illustration of b.
    - (d) b restated in other terms.
    - (e) The general principle of b illustrated from a later period in history.

    Show where these divisions occur. What is the general principle of (e)?

16. What is the relation in thought between "exaggerated" and "clerical" (l. 77)?

17. What is the difference between a characteristic and a symbol (l. 79)?

18. What is the "process" referred to in l. 86?

19. Summarize in ten words the passage "Stretches of them
. . . countryside" (ll. 47–53).

20. "pass under the hammer." Write a brief note on any
appropriate idea suggested to you by this phrase. Show
the idea that Trevelyan is seeking to drive home.

21. Give the derivation and meaning (in this extract) of moot,
turnpike, heptarchy, causeway, Pelagian, heretics,
exaggerated.

22. Learn by heart the passage "The imperial stone causeways . . . countryside" (ll. 32–53).

23. Expand the phrase "magical old English countryside"
by adding an adjectival clause (or clauses) which will
elaborate the ideas of "magical" and "old." (Do you
know anything about Merlin or Puck? Have a look at
Midsummer Night's Dream; or perhaps the magic
of the countryside calls up to you other ideas than
these.)

24. Write a short paragraph of which the first sentence is
"A few yards before me through the dusk I could see the
road rise sharply over a stone bridge."

work
for
single
effect

Your ideas are—broken arches—antiquity—sound of
trees and water — solitude — depression — haste (not
necessarily in this order, and you may, of course, add to
them).

metonymy

No. VIII

1. Green field, and glowing rock, and glancing streamlet,
all slope together in the sunshine towards the brows of
ravines, where the pines take up their own dominion of
saddened shade; and with everlasting roar in the twilight,
the stronger torrents thunder down, pale from the glaciers, 5
filling all their chasms with enchanted cold, beating themselves to pieces against the great rocks that they have
themselves cast down, and forcing fierce way beneath their
ghastly poise.

10   2. The mountain paths stoop to these glens in forky
zigzags, leading to some grey and narrow arch, all fringed
under its shuddering curve with the ferns that fear the
light; a cross of rough-hewn pine, iron-bound to its
parapet, standing dark against the lurid fury of the foam.
15 Far up the glen, as we pause beside the cross, the sky is
seen through the openings in the pines, thin with excess
of light; and, in its clear, consuming flame of white space,
the summits of the rocky mountains are gathered into
solemn crowns and circlets, all flushed in that strange,
20 faint silence of possession by the sunshine which has in it
so deep a melancholy; full of power, yet as frail as
shadows; lifeless, like the walls of a sepulcher, yet beautiful
in tender fall of crimson folds, like the veil of some sea
spirit, that lives and dies as the foam flashes; fixed on a
25 perpetual throne, stern against all strength, lifted above
all sorrow, and yet effaced and melted utterly into the air
by that last sunbeam that has crossed to them from between
the two golden clouds.

3. High above all sorrow: yes; but not unwitnessing
30 to it.   The traveler on his happy journey, as his foot
springs from the deep turf and strikes the pebbles gaily
over the edge of the mountain road, sees with a glance of
delight the clusters of nut-brown cottages that nestle
among those sloping orchards, and glow beneath the
35 boughs of the pines.   Here it may well seem to him, if
there be sometimes hardship, there must be at least
innocence and peace, and fellowship of the human soul
with nature.   It is not so.   The wild goats that leap along
those rocks have as much passion of joy in all that fair
40 work of God as the men that toil among them.   Perhaps
more.   Enter the street of one of those villages, and you
will find it foul with that gloomy foulness that is suffered
only by torpor, or by anguish of soul.   Here, it is torpor—
not absolute suffering—not starvation or disease, but
45 darkness of calm enduring; the spring known only as the

time of the scythe, and the autumn as the time of the
sickle, and the sun only as a warmth, the wind as a chill,
and the mountains as a danger. They do not understand
so much as the name of beauty, or of knowledge. They
understand dimly that of virtue. Love, patience, hospi- 50
tality, faith—these things they know. To glean their
meadows side by side, so happier; to bear the burden
up the breathless mountain flank, unmurmuringly; to
bid the stranger drink from their vessel of milk; to see at
the foot of their low deathbeds a pale figure upon a cross, 55
dying, also patiently; in this they are different from the
cattle and from the stones, but in all this unrewarded as
far as concerns the present life. For them, there is neither
hope nor passion of spirit; for them neither advance nor
exultation. Black bread, rude roof, dark night, laborious 60
day, weary arm at sunset; and life ebbs away. No
books, no thoughts, no attainments, no rest; except only
sometimes a little sitting in the sun under the church wall,
as the bell tolls thin and far in the mountain air; a
pattering of a few prayers, not understood, by the altar 65
rails of the dimly-gilded chapel, and so back to the somber
home, with the cloud upon them still unbroken—that
cloud of rocky gloom, born out of the wild torrents and
ruinous stones, and unlightened, even in their religion,
except by the vague promise of some better thing unknown, 70
mingled with threatening, and obscured by an unspeakable
horror—a smoke, as it were, of martyrdom, coiling up
with the incense, and, amidst the images of tortured bodies
and lamenting spirits in hurtling flames, the very cross,
for them, dashed more deeply than for others, with gouts of 75
blood.

4. Do not let this be thought a darkened picture of the
life of these mountaineers. It is literal fact. No contrast
can be more painful than that between the dwelling of
any well-conducted English cottager, and that of the 80
equally honest Savoyard. The one, set in the midst of its

dull, flat fields and uninteresting hedgerows, shows in itself
the love of brightness and beauty; its daisy-studded
garden-beds, its smoothly swept brick path to the
85 threshold, its freshly sanded floor and orderly shelves of
household furniture, all testify to energy of heart, and
happiness in the simple course and simple possessions of
daily life.   The other cottage, in the midst of an inconceivable, inexpressible beauty, set on some sloping bank
90 of golden sward, with clear fountains flowing beside it,
and wild flowers, and noble trees, and goodly rocks
gathered round into a perfection as of Paradise, is itself
a dark and plague-like stain in the midst of the gentle
landscape.   Within a certain distance of its threshold
95 the ground is foul and cattle-trampled; its timbers are
black with smoke, its garden choked with weeds and nameless refuse, its chambers empty and joyless, the light and
wind gleaming and filtering through the crannies of their
stones.   All testifies that to its inhabitant the world is
100 labor and vanity; that for him neither flowers bloom,
nor birds sing, nor fountains glisten; and that his soul
hardly differs from the gray cloud that coils and dies upon
his hills, except in having no fold of it touched by the
sunbeams.

JOHN RUSKIN[1]

QUESTIONS

1. Give a title to this extract.
2. Give titles to the paragraphs.
3. What is the difference between the first two and the last
   two paragraphs?
4. What is the purpose of the first two paragraphs with reference
   to the whole extract?
5. What phrase in the first paragraph contrasts with "glancing
   streamlet" (l. 1)?
6. Why "twilight" (l. 4)?

[1]Reprinted from *Modern Painters* by courtesy of George Allen & Unwin
Ltd., authorized publishers.

7. (*a*) What part of speech is "all" in "all fringed . . ." (l. 11)?

   (*b*) What is its meaning here?
8. Why "shuddering" (l. 12)?
9. Write out the adjectives and adjectival phrases that qualify "crowns and circlets"?
10. What are the "crimson folds" (l. 23)?
11. The general sense of the passage "the summits of the rocky mountains . . . golden clouds" may be explained thus: "The effect of sunlight upon the Alps is impressively beautiful but . . ." Study the passage again and again; then supply one word for the blank.
12. (*a*) What does the phrase "thin with excess of light" (l. 16) qualify?

    (*b*) Show that you understand the phenomenon to which Ruskin refers.
13. "The traveler on his happy journey . . . boughs of the pines" (ll. 30–35). How does this passage contribute to the general effect of the paragraph?
14. (*a*) What is the key-sentence of the third paragraph?

    (*b*) What does the clause "as his foot . . . mountain road" (ll. 30–32) contribute to the general effect of the passage?
15. (*a*) What single word in the third paragraph carries the idea which that paragraph mainly develops?

    (*b*) With what phrase in the fourth paragraph does it contrast?
16. What is the point in saying that they knew "the spring only as the time of the scythe, and the autumn as the time of the sickle"? What other phrases in the paragraph bring out the same idea?
17. "The sun (is known) only as a warmth." How else might it have been known?
18. "Love, patience, hospitality, faith" (l. 50). For each of these words write one phrase from this paragraph, showing how Ruskin expands the idea contained in the word.
19. "The religion of the Savoyards was a religion of . . . and of . . ." Study carefully the last part of the third paragraph and supply one word for each blank.

20. What is the exact meaning of "hurtle"?
21. Supply one word for the blank in the following: "Though to others the cross is a symbol of salvation, to the Savoyard it is a symbol of . . ."
22. What is the key-sentence of the last paragraph?
23. Why does Ruskin mention the "dull flat fields and uninteresting hedgerows" (l. 82)?
24. What phrase in the last paragraph sums up the passage "within a certain distance . . . stones" (ll. 94–99)?
25. What is the difference between "inconceivable" and "inexpressible" (l. 89)?
26. Draw up in two columns the contrasting items in the descriptions of the two homes mentioned in the fourth paragraph.
27. Summarize in forty words the passage "No contrast . . ." to the end of the paragraph.
28. Why is the refuse "nameless"?
29. Give the derivation and meaning (in this passage) of twilight, poise, enchanted, rail, martyr, sward.
30. Learn by heart the passage "The traveler . . . with nature" (ll. 30–38).
31. Write a paragraph of which the following is the first sentence: "Very striking is the contrast between the devout, scholarly monk of the medieval monastery and the worldly parson of eighteenth-century England." Develop the ideas of devotion, scholarship, and worldliness.

No. IX

1. On the greatest and most useful of all human inventions, the invention of alphabetical writing, Plato did not look with much complacency. He seems to have thought that the use of letters had operated on the human mind as the use of the go-cart in learning to walk, or of corks in learning to swim, is said to operate on the human body. It was a support which, in his opinion, soon became indispensable to those who used it, which made vigorous

exertion first unnecessary and then impossible. The
powers of the intellect would, he conceived, have been 10
more fully developed without this delusive aid. Men would
have been compelled to exercise the understanding and
the memory, and, by deep and assiduous meditation, to
make truth thoroughly their own. Now, on the contrary,
much knowledge is traced on paper, but little is engraved 15
in the soul. A man is certain that he can find information
at a moment's notice when he wants it. He therefore
suffers it to fade from his mind. Such a man cannot in
strictness be said to know anything. He has the show
without the reality of wisdom. These opinions Plato has 20
put into the mouth of an ancient king of Egypt. But it
is evident from the context that they were his own; and
so they were understood to be by Quinctilian. Indeed,
they are in perfect accordance with the whole Platonic
system.   25

2. Bacon's views, as may easily be supposed, were
widely different. The powers of the memory, he observes,
without the help of writing, can do little towards the
advancement of any useful science. He acknowledges
that the memory may be disciplined to such a point as 30
to be able to perform very extraordinary feats. But on
such feats he sets little value. The habits of his mind, he
tells us, are such that he is not disposed to rate highly any
accomplishment, however rare, which is of no practical
use to mankind. As to these prodigious achievements of 35
the memory, he ranks them with the exhibitions of rope-
dancers and tumblers. "These two performances," he
says, "are much of the same sort. The one is an abuse
of the powers of the body; the other is an abuse of the
powers of the mind. Both may perhaps excite our wonder; 40
but neither is entitled to our respect."

3. To Plato, the science of medicine appeared to be
of very disputable advantages. He did not indeed object

to quick cures for acute disorders, or for injuries produced
45 by accidents.   But the art which resists the slow sap of a
chronic disease, which repairs frames enervated by lust,
swollen by gluttony, or inflamed by wine, which encourages
sensuality by mitigating the natural punishment of the
sensualist, and prolongs existence when the intellect has
50 ceased to retain its entire energy, had no share of his
esteem.   A life protracted by medical skill he pronounced
to be a long death.   The exercise of the art of medicine
ought, he said, to be tolerated, so far as that art may
serve to cure the occasional distempers of men whose
55 constitutions are good.   As to those who have bad constitutions, let them die; and the sooner the better.   Such
men are unfit for war, for magistracy, for the management
of their domestic affairs, for severe study and speculation.
If they engage in any vigorous mental exercise, they are
60 troubled with giddiness and fulness of the head, all which
they lay to the account of philosophy.   The best thing
that can happen to such wretches is to have done with life
at once.   He quotes mythical authority in support of this
doctrine; and reminds his disciples that the practice of
65 the sons of Æsculapius, as described by Homer, extended
only to the cure of external injuries.

   4. Far different was the philosophy of Bacon. Of all
the sciences, that which he seems to have regarded with
the greatest interest was the science which, in Plato's
70 opinion, would not be tolerated in a well-regulated community.   To make men perfect was no part of Bacon's
plan.   His humble aim was to make imperfect men com-
fortable.   The beneficence of his philosophy resembled
the beneficence of the common Father, whose sun rises on
75 the evil and the good, whose rain descends for the just
and the unjust.   In Plato's opinion man was made for
philosophy; in Bacon's opinion philosophy was made
for man; it was a means to an end; and that end was to
increase the pleasures and to mitigate the pains of millions

who are not and cannot be philosophers.   That a valetudi- 80
narian who took great pleasure in being wheeled along
his terrace, who relished his boiled chicken and his weak
wine and water, and who enjoyed a hearty laugh over
the *Queen of Navarre's Tales*, should be treated as a *caput
lupinum* because he could not read the *Timaeus* without a 85
headache, was a notion which the humane spirit of the
English school of wisdom altogether rejected.   Bacon would
not have thought it beneath the dignity of a philosopher
to contrive an improved garden chair for such a valetudinarian, to devise some way of rendering his medicines more 90
palatable, to invent repasts which he might enjoy, and
pillows on which he might sleep soundly; and this though
there might not be the smallest hope that the mind of the
poor invalid would ever rise to the contemplation of the
ideal beautiful and the ideal good.   As Plato had cited 95
the religious legends of Greece to justify his contempt for
the more recondite parts of the art of healing, Bacon
vindicated the dignity of that art by appealing to the
example of Christ, and reminded men that the great
Physician of the soul did not disdain to be also the 100
physician of the body.

THOMAS BABINGTON MACAULAY

QUESTIONS

1. Give a title to this extract.
2. Give titles to the paragraphs.
3. Compare the first and third paragraphs.
4. What is the difference between Plato's attitude to alpha-
    betical writing and his attitude to the science of medicine?
5. What is antithesis? Show carefully how the question is
    suggested
        (a) by the paragraphs of this extract,
        (b) by some of the sentences.

6. Examine the first sentence of each paragraph and state its relation to the paragraph as a whole.

7. (a) Can you suggest a reason why Macaulay does not begin the first sentence of this extract with the grammatical subject?

   (b) Find in this extract two more sentences similarly constructed.

8. On five occasions in the first paragraph Macaulay reminds us that what he is saying is to be regarded as Plato's opinion. What are these occasions? Quote only the relevant part of the sentences concerned.

9. Explain in your own words the force of the analogy of the go-cart and the corks.

10. What sentences, or parts of sentences, in this extract recall the idea contained in the phrases "to exercise the understanding" and "deep and assiduous meditation"? (ll. 12–13.)

11. Show that in the third paragraph Macaulay has two ideas, both of which he expresses twice within the paragraph.

12. Why is the third sentence of the third paragraph so much more elaborated than the second sentence?

13. In what way does the end of the fourth paragraph resemble the end of the third?

14. Quote the passage which seems to you most concisely to summarize the general meaning of the whole extract.

15. Show from the fourth paragraph how Macaulay expresses an idea in a phrase and then elaborates it by giving specific examples. This is best done by writing down the phrase, underlining it, and then indicating the passage which contains the examples.

16. Possibly you may know nothing about *the Queen of Navarre's Tales, caput lupinum*, or the *Timaeus*. Study the context and make one clear statement about each that will show that at least you appreciate something of their significance.

17. Give the derivation and meaning (in this passage) of— rate, delusive, assiduous, prodigious, chronic, enervate, mitigate, speculation, valetudinarian, humane, recondite, vindicate.

18. Give the gist of the second paragraph in twenty words.

19. Learn by heart the passage "To make men perfect . . . cannot be philosophers."
20. You are writing about a cricket match. Your opponents batted first and established a first innings' lead of 130 runs. In your first innings your best batsman was injured. In the second innings the lead was increased to 408 runs and one of your most reliable batsmen sprained his thumb. There is the possibility of rain and your captain has just received a telegram containing bad news from home. Write a paragraph beginning "It was with an anxious heart that the captain watched his first pair walk to the wicket." The rest of the paragraph should be an elaboration of the word "anxious."

   If you are not interested in cricket, you may compose some other sentence containing a key-word which is to be expanded into a paragraph.

No. X

1. It seems as if a great deal were attainable in a world where there are so many marriages and decisive battles, and where we all, at certain hours of the day, and with great gusto and despatch, stow a portion of victuals finally and irretrievably into the bag which contains us. 5
And it would seem also, on a hasty view, that the attainment of as much as possible was the one goal of man's contentious life. And yet, as regards the spirit, this is but a semblance. We live in an ascending scale when we live happily, one thing leading to another in an endless 10
series. There is always a new horizon for onward-looking men, and although we dwell on a small planet, immersed in petty business and not enduring beyond a brief period of years, we are so constituted that our hopes are inaccessible, like stars, and the term of hoping is prolonged 15
until the term of life. To be truly happy is a question of

how we begin and not of how we end, of what we want
and not of what we have.   An aspiration is a joy for ever,
a possession as solid as a landed estate, a fortune which
20 we can never exhaust and which gives us year by year a
revenue of pleasurable activity.   To have many of these
is to be spiritually rich.   Life is only a very dull and
ill-directed theater unless we have some interests in the
piece; and to those who have neither art nor science,
25 the world is a mere arrangement of colors, or a rough
footway where they may very well break their shins.   It
is in virtue of his own desires and curiosities that any
man continues to exist with even patience, that he is
charmed by the look of things and people, and that he
30 wakens every morning with a renewed appetite for work
and pleasure. Desire and curiosity are the two eyes through
which he sees the world in the most enchanted colors:
it is they that make women beautiful or fossils interesting:
and the man may squander his estate and come to beggary,
35 but if he keeps these two amulets he is still rich in the
possibilities of pleasure.   Suppose he could take one meal
so compact and comprehensive that he should never
hunger any more; suppose him, at a glance, to take in
all the features of the world and allay the desire for
40 knowledge; suppose him to do the like in any province
in experience—would not that man be in a poor way
for amusement ever after?

2. One who goes touring on foot with a single volume
in his knapsack reads with circumspection, pausing often
45 to reflect, and often laying the book down to contemplate
the landscape or the prints in the inn parlor; for he
fears to come to the end of his entertainment, and be left
companionless on the last stages of his journey.   A young
fellow recently finished the works of Thomas Carlyle,
50 winding up, if we remember aright, with the ten note-books
upon Frederick the Great.   "What!" cried the young
fellow, in consternation, "is there no more Carlyle?

Am I left to the daily papers!" A more celebrated instance is that of Alexander, who wept bitterly because he had no more worlds to subdue. And when Gibbon had finished the *Decline and Fall*, he had only a few moments of joy; and it was with a "sober melancholy" that he parted from his labors.

3. Happily we all shoot at the moon with ineffectual arrows; our hopes are set on inaccessible El Dorado; we come to an end of nothing here below. Interests are only plucked up to sow themselves again, like mustard. You would think, when the child was born, there would be an end to trouble; and yet it is only the beginning of fresh anxieties; and when you have seen it through its teething and its education, and at last its marriage, alas! it is only to have new fears, new quivering sensibilities, with every day; and the health of your children's children grows as touching a concern as that of your own. Again, when you have married your wife, you would think you were got upon a hilltop, and might begin to go downward by an easy slope. But you have only ended courting to begin marriage. Falling in love and winning love are often difficult tasks to overbearing and rebellious spirits; but to keep in love is also a business of some importance, to which both man and wife must bring kindness and goodwill. The true love story commences at the altar, when there lies before the married pair a most beautiful contest of wisdom and generosity, and a life-long struggle towards an unattainable ideal. Unattainable? Ay, surely unattainable, from the very fact that they are two instead of one.

4. "Of making books there is no end," complained the Preacher; and did not perceive how highly he was praising letters as an occupation. There is no end, indeed, to making books or experiments, or to travel, or to gathering wealth. Problem gives rise to problem. We may study

for ever, and we are never as learned as we would.   We have never made a statue worthy of our dreams.   And
30 where we have discovered a continent, or crossed a chain of mountains, it is only to find another ocean or another plain upon the farther side.   In the infinite universe there is room for our swiftest diligence and to spare.   It is not like the works of Carlyle, which can be read to an end.
95 Even in a corner of it, in a private park, or in the neighborhood of a single hamlet, the weather and the seasons keep so deftly changing that although we walk there for a lifetime there will be always something new to startle and delight us.

100   5. There is only one wish realizable on the earth; only one thing that can be perfectly attained: Death. And from a variety of circumstances we have no one to tell us whether it be worth attaining.

   6. A strange picture we make on our way to our
105 Chimæras, ceaselessly marching, grudging ourselves the time for rest; indefatigable, adventurous pioneers.   It is true that we shall never reach the goal; it is even more than probable that there is no such place; and if we lived for centuries and were endowed with the powers of a god,
110 we should find ourselves not much nearer what we wanted at the end.   O toiling hands of mortals! O unwearied feet, traveling ye know not whither.   Soon, soon, it seems to you, you must come forth on some conspicuous hilltop, and but a little way farther, against the setting sun, descry
115 the spires of El Dorado.   Little do ye know your own blessedness; for to travel hopefully is a better thing than to arrive, and the true success is to labor.

                              ROBERT LOUIS STEVENSON[1]

---

[1]Reprinted from *Virginibus Puerisque* by permission of the publishers, Charles Scribner's Sons.

QUESTIONS

1. Give a title to this essay.
2. Give titles to the paragraphs.
3. In what sentence does Stevenson first state the central idea of the essay?
4. What does there appear to be common to marrying, fighting decisively, and eating?
5. What, for the purposes of Stevenson's argument, is the most significant word in the first sentence of the essay?
6. Back to what word does "semblance" (l. 9) take us?
7. For the purposes of Stevenson's argument in what way does desire resemble curiosity?
8. What is the relation between "it is they . . . that make women beautiful or fossils interesting" (l. 33) and the preceding sentence?
9. Is the passage "Suppose he could take one meal . . . ever after" (ll. 36-42) necessary for Stevenson's argument? Give a reason for your answer.
10. If you have understood the argument of the first paragraph you should be able to supply one word for each of the following blanks: "Pleasure is really an affair of the . . . not of the . . ." (Study the third sentence of the paragraph.)
11. The scope of the first paragraph might be indicated thus ". . . versus . . ." Fill these blanks with two words taken from the first paragraph.
12. What bearing has the second paragraph upon the first?
13. What feature is common to the tourist with a single volume in his knapsack, the reader of Carlyle, Alexander, and Gibbon?
14. In what way does the third paragraph differ from the second?
15. What do you notice about the thought of the first three sentences of the third paragraph?
16. Does Stevenson develop the phrases "fresh anxieties" and "new fears, new quivering sensibilities"? If so, how?
17. Compare the two passages "You would think . . . of your

own" and "Again . . . two instead of one" (ll. 63–82).
What have they in common?

18. In the fourth paragraph there is a sentence *a*, the idea
of which is expanded by means of another sentence *b*,
introducing contrast, and a third sentence *c* which gives
an illustration. What are the sentences *a*, *b*, *c*?

19. "Variety of circumstances" (l. 102). How many circumstances can you mention? Criticize the phrase.

facts,
conditions

20. Why are the adventurous pioneers (l. 106) blessed?

21. What is apostrophe? Give the derivation of the word and
show how this derivation is illustrated in the last paragraph of the essay.

22. Why is to travel hopefully a better thing than to arrive?
Answer the question by quoting one sentence from the
first paragraph.

23. Why is "descry" (l. 114) better than "see"?

24. What is the significance of the metaphor of the setting
sun (l. 114)? Perhaps the best way in which to answer
the question would be to state clearly and exactly, without any metaphor, what Stevenson means by "Soon,
soon, it seems to you . . . El Dorado."

25. Give the derivation (and meaning in this essay) of attain,
desire (you should consider very carefully the derivation
of this word and comment on its importance in this
essay), allay, pioneers, amulet.

26. Learn by heart the passage "To be truly happy . . .
and pleasure" (ll. 16–31).

27. Write two paragraphs. The first paragraph begins "Fortunately there are some things in this world that can be
attained." Develop the idea by referring in a few sentences to some of these things (*e.g.* in the world of finance,
of sport, of art, or of politics. Think, too, of some of the
humbler aims of life, the achievement of which brings
comfort). The second paragraph should be an elaboration of ideas suggested by "fortunately." What, for
example, would be the result of a permanent feeling
that attainment was beyond the lot of human beings?

No. XI

1. I stood today watching harvesters at work, and a foolish envy took hold upon me. To be one of those brawny, brown-necked men, who can string their muscles from dawn to sundown, and go home without an ache to the sound slumber which will make them fresh again for 5 tomorrow's toil! I am a man in the middle years, with limbs shaped as those of another, and subject to no prostrating malady, yet I doubt whether I could endure the lightest part of this field labor even for half an hour. Is that indeed to be a man? Could I feel surprised if one 10 of these stalwart fellows turned upon me a look of good-natured contempt? Yet he would never dream that I envied him; he would think it as probable, no doubt, that I should compare myself unfavorably with one of the farm horses.   15

2. There comes the old idle dream: balance of mind and body, perfect physical health combined with the fulness of intellectual vigor. Why should I not be there in the harvest field, if so it pleased me, yet none the less live for thought? Many a theorist holds the thing possible, 20 and looks to its coming in a better time. If so, two changes must needs come before it; there will no longer exist a profession of literature, and all but the whole of every library will be destroyed, leaving only the few books which are universally recognized as national treasures. 25 Thus, and thus only, can mental and physical equilibrium ever be brought about.

3. It is idle to talk to us of "the Greeks." The people we mean when so naming them were a few little communities, living under very peculiar conditions, and 30 endowed by Nature with most exceptional characteristics. The sporadic civilization which we are too much in the

habit of regarding as if it had been no less stable **than** brilliant, was a succession of the briefest splendors, 35 gleaming here and there from the coasts of the Ægean to those of the western Mediterranean.   Our heritage of Greek literature and art is priceless; the example of Greek life possesses for us not the slightest value.   The Greeks had nothing alien to study—not even a foreign or 40 a dead language.   They read hardly at all, preferring to listen.   They were a slave-holding people, much given to social amusement, and hardly knowing what we call industry.   Their ignorance was vast, their wisdom a grace of the gods.   Together with their fair intelligence, they 45 had grave moral weaknesses.   If we could see and speak with an average Athenian of the Periclean age, he would cause no little disappointment—there would be so much more of the barbarian in him, and at the same time of the decadent, than we had anticipated.   More than possibly, 50 even his physique would be a disillusion.   Leave him in that old world, which is precious to the imagination of a few, but to the business and bosoms of the modern multi-tude irrelevant as Memphis or Babylon.

4. The man of thought, as we understand him, is all 55 but necessarily the man of impaired health.   The rare exception will be found to come of a stock which may, indeed, have been distinguished by intelligence, but represented in all its members the active rather than the studious or contemplative life; whilst the children of 60 such fortunate thinkers are sure either to revert to the active type or to exhibit the familiar sacrifice of body to mind.   I am not denying the possibility of *mens sana in corpore sano;* that is another thing.   Nor do I speak of the healthy people (happily still numerous) who are at the 65 same time bright-witted and fond of books.   The man I have in view is he who pursues the things of the mind with passion, who turns impatiently from all common interests or cares which encroach upon his sacred time, who is

haunted by a sense of the infinity of thought and learning,
who, sadly aware of the conditions on which he holds 70
his mental vitality, cannot resist the hourly temptation
to ignore them. Add to these native characteristics the
frequent fact that such a man must make merchandise of
his attainments, must toil under the perpetual menace of
destitution; and what hope remains that his blood will 75
keep the true rhythm, that his nerves will play as Nature
bade them, that his sinews will bide the strain of exceptional
task? Such a man may gaze with envy at those who
"sweat in the eye of Phoebus," but he knows that no choice
was offered him. And if life has so far been benignant 80
as to grant him frequent tranquillity of studious hours,
let him look from the reapers to the golden harvest, and
fare on in thankfulness.

GEORGE GISSING[1]

QUESTIONS

1. Give a title to the essay.
2. Give titles to the paragraphs.
3. Why was the envy "foolish" (l. 2)? You can answer the question by quoting a sentence from another part of the essay.
4. Show that the first sentence contains a phrase the idea of which is elaborated in the second sentence.
5. "I am a man . . . malady." This may be expressed thus: "I am neither . . . nor . . . nor . . ."
   Supply one word for each blank.
6. (a) Balance of mind and body (l. 16).
   (b) Perfect physical health . . . vigor (l. 17).
   (c) Why should . . . thought (ll. 18–20).
   What is the relation in thought between (a), (b), (c)?
7. Write an answer to (c) (see 6 above) in six words, beginning "because . . ."
8. Why should anybody want to talk about the Greeks in this context (l. 28)?
9. The passage "The sporadic . . . Mediterranean" may be

---

[1]Taken by permission from Gissing's *The Private Papers of Henry Ryecroft*, published by E. P. Dutton & Co., Inc., New York.

summarized thus: "Greek civilization was . . . , . . . , and . . ."   Supply one word for each blank.

10. Why is "gleaming" (l. 35) better than "appearing"?

11. What were the chief splendors of Greek civilization?   You can answer the question by quoting a phrase from this paragraph.

12. In the light of your answer to No. 11 comment on the word "briefest" (l. 34).

13. An example is an illustration of a general rule.   What is the rule that Gissing has in mind when he speaks of "the example of Greek life"?

14. If you had to supply a connective between the sentences "the example of Greek life possesses for us not the slight-est value," and the next sentence, what connective would you use?

15. (a) "They were a slave-holding people."
    (b) "much given . . . industry" (ll. 41–43).
        What is the relation in thought between (a) and (b)?

16. Show that the phrase "a grace of the gods" has a two-fold significance.   If you cannot think of a better way, answer the question by supplying one word for each of the following blanks: "their wisdom a . . . thing . . . by the gods."   You may do it more neatly by substituting for "grace" a phrase consisting of adjective + noun.   But before answering the question study "grace" in your dictionary.

17. "The wisdom of the Greeks was a grace of the gods, but the wisdom of the moderns is the . . . of . . ."   Supply one word for each of the blanks.

18. The phrase "their fair intelligence" (l. 44) removed from its context is ambiguous.
    (a) Show that this is so.
    (b) What does "fair" mean in this context?
    (c) What phrase in the context enables you to decide?

19. Gissing indicates three reasons why the example of Greek life is valueless to us.   Give these reasons as briefly as you can under (a), (b), (c).   (Not more than half a dozen words are needed for each heading.)

20. What is the relation of the last sentence of the third paragraph ("Leave him . . .") to the whole paragraph?

21. What part of the opening sentence of the fourth paragraph leads on to the next sentence?

22. Gissing says that he is not denying the possibility of *mens sana in corpore sano* (a healthy mind in a healthy body). Then what *is* he denying? Answer the question by a phrase taken from the second paragraph, and underline the two most important words of the phrase which save Gissing from the charge of contradicting himself.

23. Why is his time "sacred" (l. 68)?

24. What, for the purposes of Gissing's argument, is the essential idea of the word "haunted" (l. 69)?

25. What are the "conditions" (l. 70)?

26. What does Gissing mean by "making merchandise of his attainments"?

27. Give in twenty words the meaning of the passage "The man I have in view . . . to ignore them" (ll. 65–72), and give it as title "The . . . of Knowledge." Fill the blank with a noun indicating the man.

28. Somebody, asked to substitute other words for "sweat in the eye of Phoebus," wrote "work hard."
    (*a*) Criticize the answer.
    (*b*) What words would *you* substitute to bring out the full idea?

29. Why was no choice offered him (l. 79)?
    (*a*) "Because he . . .": complete by quoting from this paragraph.
    (*b*) Choice between what?

30. Study very thoughtfully the words "let him look from the reapers to the golden harvest, and fare on in thankfulness."
    (*a*) What does Gissing mean by the "golden harvest"?
    (*b*) Why should the man of thought be thankful?

31. Compare the first and last sentences of this essay. What interesting difference do you notice?

32. Give the derivation and meaning (in this essay) of string—stalwart—equilibrium—peculiar (what has "cattle" got to do with it?)—sporadic—alien—illusion—passion—rhythm (why is the word so appropriate in this context?)—strain (what word in the first paragraph is connected in derivation with this?)—studious.

33. Learn by heart the passage "The man I have in mind
    . . . in thankfulness" (ll. 65-end).

34. Write a paragraph in which you protest that you are being
    overworked. Show in detail how your studies have
    encroached on your time for recreation. Dwell on the
    penalties of ill-health (*e.g.* in sport, business, social life,
    etc.). Your first sentence is, "I am compelled to devote
    too much time to study, and my health is suffering in
    consequence."

    (Does it interest you to learn that the Greek word
    which gives us "school," means "leisure"? If it does,
    work some allusion into your paragraph.)

No. XII

1. Bodily labor is of two kinds, either that which a
man submits to for his livelihood, or that which he undergoes for his pleasure. The latter of them generally changes
the name of labor for that of exercise, but differs only
5 from ordinary labor as it rises from another motive.

2. A country life abounds in both these kinds of labor,
and for that reason gives a man a greater stock of health,
and consequently a more perfect enjoyment of himself,
than any other way of life. I consider the body as a system
10 of tubes and glands, or to use a more rustic phrase, a
bundle of pipes and strainers, fitted to one another after
so wonderful a manner as to make a proper engine for the
soul to work with. This description does not only comprehend the bowels, bones, tendons, veins, nerves, and
15 arteries, but every muscle and every ligature, which is a
composition of fibers, that are so many imperceptible
tubes or pipes interwoven on all sides with invisible glands
or strainers.

3. This general idea of a human body, without con-

sidering it in its niceties of anatomy, lets us see how abso- 20
lutely necessary labor is for the right preservation of it.
There must be frequent motions and agitations, to mix,
digest, and separate the juices contained in it, as well as
to clear and cleanse that infinitude of pipes and strainers
of which it is composed, and to give their solid parts a 25
more firm and lasting tone.   Labor or exercise ferments
the humors, casts them into their proper channels, throws
off redundancies, and helps nature in those secret distri-
butions, without which the body cannot subsist in its
vigor, nor the soul act with cheerfulness.   30

4. I might here mention the effects which this has upon
all the faculties of the mind, by keeping the understanding
clear, the imagination untroubled, and refining those
spirits that are necessary for the proper exertion of our
intellectual faculties, during the present laws of union 35
between soul and body.   It is to a neglect in this particular
that we must ascribe the spleen, which is so frequent in
men of studious and sedentary tempers, as well as the
vapors to which those of the other sex are so often
subject.   40

5. Had not exercise been absolutely necessary for our
well-being, nature would not have made the body so proper
for it, by giving such an activity to the limbs, and such a
pliancy to every part as necessarily produce these com-
pressions, extensions, contortions, dilatations, and all 45
other kinds of motions that are necessary for the preservation of such a system of tubes and glands as has been
before mentioned.   And that we might not want induce-
ments to engage us in such an exercise of the body as is
proper for its welfare, it is so ordered that nothing valuable 50
can be procured without it.   Not to mention riches and
honor, even food and raiment are not to be come at
without the toil of the hands and sweat of the brows.
Providence furnishes materials, but expects that we should

55 work them up ourselves. The earth must be labored
before it gives its increase, and when it is forced into its
several products, how many hands must they pass through
before they are fit for use? Manufactures, trade, and
agriculture, naturally employ more than nineteen parts
60 of the species in twenty; and as for those who are not
obliged to labor, by the condition in which they are born,
they are more miserable than the rest of mankind, unless
they indulge themselves in that voluntary labor which
goes by the name of exercise.

65 6. My friend Sir Roger has been an indefatigable man
in business of this kind, and has hung several parts of his
house with the trophies of his former labors. The walls
of his great hall are covered with the horns of several
kinds of deer that he has killed in the chase, which he
70 thinks the most valuable furniture of his house, as they
afford him frequent topics of discourse, and show that he
has not been idle. At the lower end of the hall is a large
otter's skin stuffed with hay, which his mother ordered
to be hung up in that manner, and the Knight looks upon it
75 with great satisfaction, because it seems he was but nine
years old when his dog killed him. A little room adjoining
to the hall is a kind of arsenal filled with guns of several
sizes and inventions, with which the Knight has made
great havoc in the woods, and destroyed many thousand
80 of pheasants, partridges, and woodcocks. His stable doors
are patched with noses that belonged to foxes of the Knight's
own hunting down. Sir Roger showed me one of them, that
for distinction sake has a brass nail struck through it,
which cost him about fifteen hours' riding, carried him
85 through half a dozen counties, killed him a brace of geld-
ings, and lost above half his dogs. This the Knight looks
upon as one of the greatest exploits of his life. The perverse widow, whom I have given some account of, was
the death of several foxes; for Sir Roger has told me that
90 in the course of his amours he patched the western door

of his stable. Whenever the widow was cruel, the foxes
were sure to pay for it. In proportion as his passion for
the widow abated, and old age came on, he left off fox-
hunting; but a hare is not yet safe that sits within ten
miles of his house.   95

7. There is no kind of exercise which I would so rec-
ommend to my readers of both sexes as this of riding, as
there is none which so much conduces to health, and is
every way accommodated to the body, according to the
idea which I have given of it. Doctor Sydenham is very 100
lavish in its praises; and if the English reader will see
the mechanical effects of it described at length, he may
find them in a Book published not many years since, under
the title of *Medicina Gymnastica*. For my own part,
when I am in town, for want of these opportunities, I 105
exercise myself an hour every morning upon a dumb bell
that is placed in a corner of my room, and pleases me the
more because it does everything I require of it in the most
profound silence. My landlady and her daughters are so
well acquainted with my hours of exercise, that they never 110
come into my room to disturb me whilst I am ringing.

8. When I was some years younger than I am at present,
I used to employ myself in a more laborious diversion,
which I learned from a Latin treatise of exercises that is
written with great erudition: It is there called the σχιουαχία 115
or the fighting with a man's own shadow, and consists
in the brandishing of two short sticks grasped in each
hand, and loaden with plugs of lead at either end. This
opens the chest, exercises the limbs, and gives a man all
the pleasure of boxing, without the blows. I could wish 120
that several learned men would lay out that time which
they employ in controversies and disputes about nothing,
in this method of fighting with their own shadows. It
might conduce very much to evaporate the spleen, which
makes them uneasy to the public as well as to themselves. 125

9. To conclude, as I am a compound of soul and body, I consider myself as obliged to a double scheme of duties; and think I have not fulfilled the business of the day, when I do not thus employ the one in labor and exercise, ₁₃₀ as well as the other in study and contemplation.

JOSEPH ADDISON

QUESTIONS

1. Give a title to this essay.
2. Give titles to the paragraphs.
3. Do you think that the word "only" is justifiable in l. 4? Give a reason for your answer.
4. What is the difference between a motive and a cause?
5. (a) Of the phrases "A system of tubes and glands," and "a proper engine for the soul to work with," which do you think most suitably indicates the scope of the second paragraph?
   (b) Consider the phrase you reject and explain why you reject it.
   (c) Why is "system of tubes, etc." better than "bundle of tubes, etc."?
6. (a) What is the difference between veins and arteries?
   (b) To what does "their" (l. 25) refer?
   (c) What are the "solid parts"?
7. Give the gist of the third paragraph in not more than six words.
8. What idea is common to "clear," "untroubled," and "refining"?
9. There is much about the laws of union between soul and body of which we know nothing. But in the light of this essay you should be able to enunciate one of these laws. What is it?
10. Divide the fifth paragraph into three sections, indicating as briefly as possible the idea of each section.
11. Show that in the fifth paragraph Addison uses the word "exercise" in two different senses.
12. What is the essential difference for the purposes of Addison's

argument between riches and honor, on the one hand, and food and raiment, on the other?

13. Why is the phrase "not to be come at" better than "not to be obtained"?

14. Is the "voluntary labor which goes by the name of exercise" an indulgence, or a necessity? Think carefully before you answer.

15. How does the sixth paragraph contribute to the essay as a whole? For example, does it advance the argument?

16. What is the key-phrase of the sixth paragraph?

17. What single word in the first three lines of the sixth paragraph takes us back in thought to the last sentence of the fifth paragraph?

18. Can you suggest any reason why Sir Roger, when he was tormented by his fruitless love of the perverse widow, chose fox-hunting in preference to the other forms of sport mentioned?

19. Quote two short passages from the sixth paragraph to show the simplicity of Sir Roger's character.

20. In what way do the last four paragraphs of this essay differ markedly from the first five paragraphs?

21. What is the "idea which I have given of it" (l. 100)?

22. What is there about the controversies and disputes mentioned in l. 122 to suggest that this particular method of exercise is appropriate?

23. What is the most vivid passage in the essay?

24. Give the derivation and meaning (in this essay) of system, faculties, niceties, spleen, sedentary, vapors, indefatigable, brandishing.

25. Summarize in forty words Addison's argument in support of bodily labor.

26. Learn by heart the fourth paragraph as far as ". . . soul and body."

27. Write a paragraph (20-30 lines) of which this is the last sentence—"Thus Nature herself teaches us that over-indulgence in bodily exercise is harmful both to body and to mind." (Consider very carefully the last seven words.)

No. XIII

1. What is war? I believe that half the people that
talk about war have not the slightest idea of what it is.
In a short sentence it may be summed up to be the combination and concentration of all the horrors, atrocities,
5 crimes, and sufferings of which human nature on this globe
is capable. But what is even a rumor of war? Is there
anybody here who has anything in the funds, or who is
the owner of any railway stock, or anybody who has a
large stock of raw material or manufactured goods?
10 The funds have recently gone down 10 per cent. I do not
say that the fall is all on account of this danger of war,
but a great proportion of it undoubtedly is. A fall of
10 per cent in the funds is nearly £80,000,000 sterling of
value, and railway stock having gone down 20 per
15 cent makes a difference of £60,000,000 in the value of
the railway property of this country. Add the two—
£140,000,000—and take the diminished prosperity and
value of manufactures of all kinds during the last few
months, and you will understate the actual loss to the
20 country now if you put it down at £200,000,000 sterling.
But that is merely a rumor of war. That is war a long
way off—the small cloud, no bigger than a man's hand—
what will it be if it comes nearer and becomes a fact?
And surely sane men ought to consider whether the case
25 is a good one, the ground fair, the necessity clear, before
they drag a nation of nearly 30,000,000 of people into a
long and bloody struggle, for a decrepit and tottering
empire, which all the nations in Europe cannot long
sustain. And, mind, war now would take a different
30 aspect from what it did formerly. It is not only that you
send out men who submit to be slaughtered, and that you
pay a large amount of taxes—the amount of taxes would
be but a feeble indication of what you would suffer.
Our trade is now much more extensive than it was; our

commerce is more expanded, our undertakings are more 35
vast, and war will find you all out at home by withering
up the resources of the prosperity enjoyed by the middle
and working classes of the country. You would find that
war in 1853 would be infinitely more perilous and destructive to our country than it has ever yet been at any former 40
period of our history. There is another question which
comes home to my mind with a gravity and seriousness
which I can scarcely hope to communicate to you. You
who lived during the period from 1815 to 1822 may remember that this country was probably never in a more 45
uneasy position. The sufferings of the working classes
were beyond description, and the difficulties and struggles
and bankruptcies of the middle classes were such as few
persons have a just idea of. There was scarcely a year in
which there was not an incipient insurrection in some parts 50
of the country, arising from the sufferings which the
working classes endured. You know very well that the
Government of the day employed spies to create plots,
and to get ignorant men to combine to take unlawful
oaths; and you know that in the town of Stirling, two men 55
who, but for this diabolical agency, might have lived good
and honest citizens, paid the penalty of their lives for their
connection with unlawful combinations of this kind.

2. Well, if you go into war now you will have more
banners to decorate your cathedrals and churches. 60
Englishmen will fight now as well as they ever did, and
there is ample power to back them if the country can be
but sufficiently excited and deluded. You may raise up
great generals. You may have another Wellington, and
another Nelson too; for this country can grow men 65
capable for every enterprise. Then there may be titles,
and pensions, and marble monuments to eternize the men
who have thus become great; but what becomes of you,
and your country, and your children? For there is more
than this in store. That seven years to which I have 70

referred was a period dangerous to the existence of **Govern-** ment in this country, for the whole substratum, the whole foundations of society were discontented, suffering intolerable evils, and hostile in the bitterest degree to the 75 institutions and the Government of the country.

3. Precisely the same things will come again.   Rely on it, that injustice of any kind, be it bad laws, or be it a bloody, unjust, and unnecessary war, of necessity creates perils to every institution in the country.   If the Corn Law 80 had continued, if it had been impossible, by peaceful agitation, to abolish it, the monarchy itself would not have survived the ruin and disaster that it must have wrought. And if you go into a war now, with a doubled population, with a vast commerce, with extended credit, and a wider 85 diffusion of partial education among the people, let there ever come a time like the period between 1815 and 1822, when the whole basis of society is upheaving with a sense of intolerable suffering, I ask you, how many years' purchase would you give even for the venerable and mild 90 monarchy under which you have the happiness to live? I confess when I think of the tremendous perils into which unthinking men—men who do not intend to fight them- selves—are willing to drag or to hurry this country, I am amazed how they can trifle with interests so vast, and 95 consequences so much beyond their calculation.

4. But, speaking here in Edinburgh to such an audience —an audience probably for its numbers as intelligent and as influential as ever was assembled within the walls of any hall in this kingdom—I think I may put before you 100 higher considerations even than those of property and the institutions of your country.   I may remind you of duties more solemn, and of obligations more imperative.   You profess to be a Christian nation.   You make it your boast even—though boasting is somewhat out of place in such 105 questions—you make it your boast that you are **a**

Protestant people, and that you draw your rule of doctrine and practice, as from a well, pure and undefiled, from the living oracles of God, and from the direct revelation of the Omnipotent. You have even conceived the magnificent project of illuminating the whole earth, even to its remotest 110 and darkest recesses, by the dissemination of the volume of the New Testament, in whose every page are written for ever the words of peace. Within the limits of this island alone, on every Sabbath, 20,000—yes, far more than 20,000 —temples are thrown open, in which devout men and 115 women assemble that they may worship Him who is the "Prince of Peace."

5. Is this a reality? or is your Christianity a romance? is your profession a dream? No, I am sure that your Christianity is not a romance, and I am equally sure that 120 your profession is not a dream. It is because I believe this that I appeal to you with confidence, and that I have hope and faith in the future. I believe that we shall see, and at no very distant time, sound economic principles spreading much more widely amongst the people; a sense 125 of justice growing up in a soil which hitherto has been deemed unfruitful; and, which will be better than all— the Churches of the United Kingdom—the Churches of Britain—awaking, as it were, from their slumbers, and girding up their loins to more glorious work, when they 130 shall not only accept and believe in the prophecy, but labor earnestly for its fulfilment, that there shall come a time—a blessed time—a time which shall last for ever— when "nation shall not lift up sword against nation, neither shall they learn war any more." 35

JOHN BRIGHT

QUESTIONS

1. Give a title to this speech.
2. Give titles to the paragraphs.

3. What is the part played by the first three sentences in the first paragraph as a whole?

4. What is the key-sentence of the first paragraph?

5. Divide the first paragraph into four sections, and as briefly as possible (by single words or by phrases) indicate the scope of each section.

6. "But what is even a rumor of war?" What single sentence in the paragraph answers this question?

7. What are "the funds" (l. 10)?

8. In the passage "Is there anybody . . . £200,000,000 sterling" (ll. 6–20) Bright appeals to the . . . instincts of his audience. Supply one word for the blank.

9. What is the loss to the sentence if you put the subordinate clause "if you put it down at £200,000,000 sterling" in front of the main clause?

10. "What will it be if it comes nearer and becomes a fact?" (l. 23.) What single sentence in the paragraph answers this question?

11. Does "our commerce is more expanded" (l. 35) add to the thought of the preceding statement? You will have to consider whether Bright implies a difference between *trade* and *commerce*.

12. (a) What exactly are the "resources" (l. 37)?
    (b) How are they withered up by war?

13. What is the exact significance of "comes home to" (l. 42)? Show that it is better than "occurs to."

14. Illustrate from the first paragraph the way in which Bright states an idea in general terms, and then in subsequent sentences expands and illustrates that idea.

15. What is the precise significance of Bright's reference to "banners" in l. 60?

16. "An idea is often made more impressive by being brought into contrast with its opposite." Illustrate this dictum from the second paragraph.

17. What is the connection in thought between "excited" and "deluded" (l. 63)?

18. What is the key-sentence of the second paragraph?

19. The gist of the sentence "Then there may be . . . become great" (ll. 66–68) may be given in the phrase ". . . of great men." Supply one word for the blank.

20. What effect would be lost if the sentence cited above in No. 19 were inserted immediately after the first sentence of the paragraph?

21. "More than this" (l. 69).
    (a) More than what?
    (b) Substitute for "this" a single noun.

22. Show carefully what relation the third and fourth sentences of the third paragraph bear to the second sentence of that paragraph?

23. Examine the fourth sentence of the third paragraph. What is the purpose of the words "I ask you"?

24. What bearing has "partial education" (l. 85) upon Bright's argument?

25. What does Bright mean by "how many years' purchase" (l. 88)? What is the origin of the phrase?

26. In what way do the adjectives "venerable and mild" contribute to Bright's argument?

27. What is the key-sentence of the fourth paragraph?

28. What rhetorical devices can you discover in the last two paragraphs?

29. How does Bright emphasize the word "whole" (l. 110)?

30. Give in thirty words the gist of Bright's argument in the fourth paragraph.

31. What passage in the last paragraph picks up and emphasizes the ideas contained in the phrase "doctrine and practice" (l. 106)?

32. Study the first paragraph, and then cite one sound economic principle.

33. Were there any circumstances under which Bright would sanction warfare? Support your opinion by quoting from this speech.

34. Give the derivation and meaning (in this speech) of communicate, incipient, solemn, obligations, dissemination, economic, oracle, romance.

35. Learn by heart the passage "I may remind you . . . words of peace" (ll. 101–113).

36. Prepare notes for a speech urging a crowd of British workmen to refrain from striking; write out in full the second paragraph of that speech; and show how you would organize your notes for the other paragraphs.

No. XIV

1. This House today desires to pay tribute to one who
was a Member of this House for more than a generation.
He was essentially a House of Commons man, and he was
perhaps one of the greatest Parliamentarians of the last
5 century.   For that task his equipment was, indeed, remarkable and complete: an intellect fine and rare, trained
in those schools best calculated to bring out the noblest
qualities of that type of intellect; a scholar steeped in
the classical tradition, with a profound knowledge of the
10 literature of his own country, and a speaker of his own
tongue, I think I may say, without rival in his generation.
His speeches as they fell from his lips were literature,
and, though few things are so ephemeral as the spoken
word, I am convinced that generations yet to come will
15 read his speeches in the early days of the War and the
tribute he paid in this House to Alfred Lyttelton, one of
the most beautiful tributes to a loved Member of this
House that has ever been paid.

2. With him, every word as he spoke fell into its place
20 inevitably.   There was no meretricious adornment.   There
was not one excessive word.   His argument was close-
reasoned and logical, and his whole speech compact together as if fitted in the brain of a master.   His judgment,
helped by his temperament, which was essentially calm
25 and judicial, was rarely at fault.   I think few leaders in
this House made fewer mistakes than he in judging the
temper either of his party or the House.   He had a profound knowledge of both, and he maintained a poise in all
matters connected with this House and politically that
30 nothing upset and that nothing ruffled.   His personal
integrity was unassailable, his loyalty to those whom he
served or those who served him never failed.   It was a
loyalty deep set, built into his character, that wrought no

evil and that thought no evil, and with that a nature large
and magnanimous, which never harbored a mean thought. 35
He was always ready to let others have credit. He was
always ready to take the blame that belonged to others
on to his own shoulders.

3. Keen controversialist and strong party man as he
was, I look back on those half-dozen years immediately 40
preceding the War, when there was more bitterness in
political controversy than there had been for a generation
before, or has been since, and I can remember no instance
in which, whether on the platform or in this House, he
spoke words that were false or words that could wound. 45
Such wounds as he inflicted in political conflict were wounds
that were caused in his opponents by the closeness of his
logic and the weight of his arguments. No malice ever
entered into them. In politics he showed that magnanimity which we often feel, I hope rightly, is the peculiar 50
possession of our race in its political life. Under an
exterior sometimes brusque in this House, there was a
very tender, human heart, well known to his friends, and
it is little wonder not only that he won admiration, an
admiration due to his gifts in this House, but that he won 55
a much rarer thing, the love of those who worked with him
as of those who were his friends.

4. Public life tries character as by fire. It tries it in
success, and it tries it in the moment of what the world
calls failure. There were some words which he wrote 60
as far back as 1910, at the close of an address to the students
of Aberdeen, which I think explain his outlook on life in
the face of success and of failure:

5. "Keep always with you, wherever your course may
lie, the company of great thoughts, the inspiration of 65
great ideals, the example of great achievements, the
consolation of great failures. So equipped, you can face

without perturbation the buffets of circumstance, the caprice of fortune, or the inscrutable vicissitudes of life."

70 6. Though, perhaps, temptations come more subtly and are less easily discernible to men who walk in the high places of this earth, the deterioration of character which has so often been seen in this world is more obvious to mankind when men have to face bitter and cruel
75 disappointments. In the last years of his life he had to face such, and he faced them without bitterness, without blame, without self-pity, and with no attempt at self-justification. He faced them with a dignity perfect and restrained, and towards the closing years of his life, as
80 throughout his life, but never more than in those closing years, he conferred distinction on the public life of this country and distinction on this House which he had known for so long.

7. His voice is silent today. A few years, and there
85 will be none who will remember it. A few years, and the voices of those addressing the House today will be silent, too, and a few more years and their voices will be forgotten. But the character and the spirit remain to fortify the coming generations and to illuminate their paths. We
90 turn aside today for a moment from controversy and from business, and, as we leave this Chamber, we shall leave it for this afternoon to darkness and to silence. Into that darkness and into that silence we must all go when our time comes. May it be our lot to leave behind to our friends
95 as fragrant a memory as Lord Oxford, and to our country a light, however faint, to lighten the steps of those who come after.   STANLEY BALDWIN[1]

QUESTIONS

1. Give a title to this speech.
2. Give titles to the paragraphs.

[1]Reprinted from *On England* by permission of the publishers, Frederick A. Stokes Company.

3. The passage "With him, every word . . . of a master" (ll. 19–23) deals with Lord Oxford as a speaker, and you might argue that it should come in the first paragraph. Defend its right to appear in the second paragraph.

4. What three words in the first paragraph amplify the word "equipment" (l. 5)?

5. (a) What is the meaning of the phrase "steeped in the classical tradition"? Try to bring out the full force of "steeped."

   (b) With what may the phrase be contrasted in this context?

6. We may divide the second paragraph into two parts:
   (a) . . . qualities; (b) . . . qualities.
   Show where the division in the paragraph occurs and supply one word for each of the blanks above.

7. Show that the third paragraph contains ideas that have already been presented in the second paragraph.

8. What relation does the sentence "In politics he showed . . . political life" (ll. 49–51) bear to the whole paragraph?

9. Quote from the third paragraph a sentence containing antithesis and underline only the words that indicate the antithetical ideas.

10. In what three ways did Lord Oxford show his magnanimity?

11. (a) Compare the first sentence of the fourth paragraph with the first sentence of the sixth.

    (b) What word in the sixth paragraph suggests the comparison? Comment on its derivation. temptation

12. Consider the passage "In the last years of his life . . . perfect and restrained" (ll. 75–79) and show how the speaker emphasizes in two different ways the fortitude of Lord Oxford.

13. Note the phrase "a dignity perfect and restrained." Why are the adjectives placed after the noun? Quote from this speech another example of a noun qualified by two following adjectives.

14. Comment upon the position in its sentence of the phrase "Into that darkness and into that silence."

15. In the last paragraph what two ideas are contrasted? physical & spiritual

16. "Illuminate their paths" (l. 89). Where else in this paragraph is the same idea expressed?

final summing up of an argument *eulogy*

17. What is a peroration? Illustrate from the closing paragraph the characteristic features of a peroration.

18. The name of the subject of this panegyric is held over until the last sentence. Why is this? *concentrate more in the qualities*

19. This extract illustrates two different uses of the colon. What are they?

20. Give the derivation and meaning (in this speech) of—fine, ephemeral, meretricious, compact (what other word in this sentence contains a very similar idea?) integrity, magnanimous, harbored (what is there peculiar in the use of this word?), caprice (what has the goat got to do with it?), inscrutable, vicissitudes, controversialist.

21. Learn by heart the last paragraph.

22. Summarize in twenty words the passage "Keen controversialist . . . entered into them" (ll. 38–49).

23. The last day of your last term at school is over. You have done with your school books. In the privacy of your study or of the empty classroom, you have just delivered "A Farewell Speech to My Books." Write the peroration (one paragraph) of this speech. If you can't think of a better, your opening sentence might be: "And so, my books, I bid you farewell."

No. XV

1. The motives that may engage a wise prince or state in a war I take to be one or more of these: either to check the overgrown power of some ambitious neighbor; to recover what has been unjustly taken from them; to
5 revenge some injury they have received, which all political casuists allow; to assist some ally in a just quarrel; or, lastly, to defend themselves when they are invaded. In all these cases the writers upon politics admit a war to be justly undertaken. The last is, what has been usually
10 called *pro aris et focis;* where no expense or endeavor can be too great, because all we have is at stake, and consequently our utmost force to be exerted; and the

dispute is soon determined, either in safety or utter destruction. But in the other four I believe it will be found that no monarch or commonwealth did ever engage 15 beyond a certain degree: never proceeding so far as to exhaust the strength and substance of their country by anticipations and loans, which in a few years must put them in a worse condition than any they could reasonably apprehend from those evils for the preventing of which 20 they first entered into the war; because this would be to run into real infallible ruin, only in hopes to remove what might perhaps but appear so by a probable speculation.

2. And as a war should be undertaken upon a just and prudent motive, so it is still more obvious that a prince 25 ought naturally to consider the condition he is in when he enters on it; whether his coffers be full, his revenues clear of debts, his people numerous and rich by a long peace and free trade, not overpressed with many burdensome taxes; no violent faction ready to dispute his just pre- 30 rogative, and thereby weaken his authority at home and lessen his reputation abroad. For if the contrary of all this happen to be his case he will hardly be persuaded to disturb the world's quiet and his own, while there is any other way left of preserving the latter with honor and 35 safety.

3. Supposing the war to have commenced upon a just motive, the next thing to be considered is, when a prince ought in prudence to receive the overtures of a peace; which I take to be, either when the enemy is ready to 40 yield the point originally contended for, or when that point is found impossible to be ever obtained; or when contending any longer, although with probability of gaining that point at last, would put such a prince and his people in a worse condition than the present loss of it. All which 45 considerations are of much greater force where a war is managed by an alliance of many confederates, which, in

a variety of interests among the several parties, is liable
to so many unforeseen accidents.

50   4. In a confederate war it ought to be considered which
party has the deepest share in the quarrel: for, although
each may have their particular reasons, yet one or two
among them will probably be more concerned than the
rest, and therefore ought to bear the greatest part of the
55 burden, in proportion to their strength.   For example:
two princes may be competitors for a kingdom; and it
will be your interest to take the part of him who will
probably allow you good conditions of trade, rather than
of the other who may possibly not.   However, that prince
60 whose cause you espouse, although never so vigorously,
is the principal in that war, and you, properly speaking,
are but a second.   Or a commonwealth may lie in danger
to be overrun by a powerful neighbor, which in time
may produce very bad consequences upon your trade
65 and liberty: it is therefore necessary, as well as prudent,
to lend them assistances, and help them to win a strong,
secure frontier; but, as they must, in course, be the first
and greatest sufferers, so, in justice, they ought to bear
the greatest weight.   If a house be on fire, it behoves all
70 in the neighborhood to run with buckets to quench it,
but the owner is sure to be undone first; and it is not
impossible that those at next door may escape by a shower
from Heaven, or the stillness of the weather, or some other
favorable accident.

75   5. But if any ally, who is not so immediately concerned
in the good or ill fortune of the war, be so generous as to
contribute more than the principal party, and even more in
proportion to his abilities, he ought at least to have his
share in what is conquered from the enemy; or, if his
80 romantic disposition transport him so far as to expect
little or nothing from this, he might, however, hope that
the principals would make it up in dignity and respect;

and he would surely think it monstrous to find them inter-
meddling in his domestic affairs, prescribing what servants
he should keep or dismiss, pressing him perpetually with 85
the most unreasonable demands, and at every turn
threatening to break the alliance if he will not comply.

6. From these reflections upon war in general I descend
to consider those wars wherein England has been engaged
since the Conquest. In the civil wars of the barons, as 90
well as those between the houses of York and Lancaster,
great destruction was made of the nobility and gentry;
new families raised, and old ones extinguished; but the
money spent on both sides was employed and circulated
at home; no public debts contracted, and a very few 95
years of peace quickly set all right again.

7. The like may be affirmed even of that unnatural
rebellion against King Charles I. The usurpers maintained
great armies in constant pay, had almost continual war
with Spain or Holland; but managing it by their fleets, 100
they increased very much the riches of the kingdom,
instead of exhausting them.

8. Our foreign wars were generally against Scotland
or France; the first, being in this island, carried no money
out of the kingdom, and were seldom of long continuance. 105
During our first wars with France we possessed great
dominions in that country, where we preserved some
footing till the reign of Queen Mary; and although some
of our later princes made very chargeable expeditions
thither, a subsidy and two or three fifteenths[1] cleared all 110
the debt. Besides, our victories were then of some use
as well as glory; for we were so prudent as to fight, and
so happy as to conquer, only for ourselves.

9. The Dutch wars in the reign of King Charles II,

---

[1] *Fifteenth:* Originally a tax of $\frac{1}{15}$ of the value of movable property.

115 although begun and carried on under a very corrupt administration, and much to the dishonor of the Crown, did indeed keep the king needy and poor by discontinuing or discontenting his Parliament when he most needed their assistance; but neither left any debt upon the 120 nation, nor carried any money out of it.

10. At the Revolution a general war broke out in Europe, wherein many princes joined in alliance against France, to check the ambitious designs of that monarch; and here the emperor, the Dutch, and England, were principals. 125 About this time the custom first began among us of borrowing millions upon funds of interest. It was pretended that the war could not possibly last above one or two campaigns; and that the debts contracted might be easily paid in a few years by a gentle tax, without 130 burdening the subject. But the true reason for embracing this expedient was the security of a new prince, not firmly settled on the throne. People were tempted to lend by great premiums and large interest; and it concerned them nearly to preserve that government which they had 135 trusted with their money. The person said to have been author of so detestable a project lived to see some of its fatal consequences, whereof his grandchildren will not see an end. And this pernicious counsel closed very well with the posture of affairs at that time: for a set of upstarts, 140 who had little or no part in the Revolution, but valued themselves upon their noise and pretended zeal when the work was over, were got into credit at court, by the merit of becoming undertakers and projectors of loans and funds; these, finding that the gentlemen of estates were not willing 145 to come into their measures, fell upon those new schemes of raising money, in order to create a moneyed interest that might in time vie with the landed, and of which they hoped to be at the head.

11. The ground of the first war for ten years after the

Revolution, as to the part we had in it, was to make 150
France acknowledge the late king, and to recover Hudson's
Bay. But during that whole war the sea was almost
entirely neglected, and the greatest part of six millions
annually employed to enlarge the frontier of the Dutch;
for the king was a general, but not an admiral, and, al- 155
though king of England, was a native of Holland.

12. After ten years' fighting to little purpose, after the
loss of above a hundred thousand men, and a debt remain-
ing of twenty millions, we at length hearkened to the terms
of peace, which was concluded with great advantages to 160
the empire and Holland, but none at all to us, and clogged
soon after with the famous treaty of partition.

JONATHAN SWIFT

QUESTIONS

1. Give a title to this extract.
2. Give titles to the paragraphs.
3. At what point would you divide this extract into two
   sections?
4. Show how Swift in stating the five motives that may lead
   to a just war, indicates in each statement, by word or
   by clause, the justice of that war.
5. The *Pocket Oxford Dictionary* defines a casuist as a "person
   who examines special cases as affected by conflicting
   moral rules." What are the moral rules involved in the use
   of the word *casuist* in l. 6?
6. In the passage "where no expense . . . exerted" (ll. 10–12)
   what phrases echo the thought of "expense" and "endeavor"?
7. Give *one* word that may be substituted for the phrase
   "monarch or commonwealth" (l. 15).
8. "No monarch . . . degree." With what clause in the
   paragraph is this brought into contrast?
9. "Never proceeding so far . . . into the war" (ll. 16–21).

What is the relation between this and the preceding
sentence?

10. Substitute a phrase for the word "this" (l. 21). Your
phrase must fit neatly, grammatically, and logically into
the sentence.

11. Show how in the second paragraph Swift sets out a general
idea which he afterwards elaborates by means of detailed
considerations.

12. In what way does the reference to "the world's quiet"
(l. 34) strengthen Swift's argument in the second paragraph?

13. To what two adjectives respectively are we taken back in
thought by "long peace" and "free trade" (ll. 28–29)?

14. The passage "either when the enemy . . . loss of it"
(ll. 40–45) may be summarized thus: "When the war
can no longer . . . be waged." Supply one word for
the blank.

15. Why are "considerations" mentioned in l. 46 of much
greater force where a war is managed by an alliance of
many confederates? The answer is suggested by a
phrase of four words to be found in this paragraph.

16. What is an analogy? How does the question arise from a
study of the fourth paragraph?

17. (a) What point have the three examples mentioned in the
fourth paragraph got in common?

    (b) What phrases in the second and third examples of the
    fourth paragraph correspond to the phrase "the
    principal in that war"?

    (c) How does the last sentence of the fourth paragraph
    contribute to Swift's argument?

18. What is the difference between "contributing more" and
"contributing more in proportion to one's abilities"?

19. "romantic disposition" (l. 80). What words in the context justify the adjective "romantic"? Give a synonym
for "romantic."

20. Supply one word for the blank in "He might, however,
hope that the principals would . . . him in dignity and
respect."

21. Why is "prescribing" (l. 84) better than "recommend-
ing"?

22. Summarize the fifth paragraph in 35–40 words.
23. Substitute a short noun phrase for "it" in l. 82. If you rewrite the sentence with this noun phrase in place of it, what other change will you have to make?
24. Of what is the passage "and he would surely think it, monstrous . . . comply" (ll. 83–87) an expansion?
25. (a) What characteristic is common to all the wars mentioned in paragraphs 6, 7, 8, 9?
    (b) Where else in the extract is this characteristic indicated?
26. In what respect do the sixth, seventh, eighth, and ninth paragraphs differ from the last three paragraphs of the extract?
27. What is the key-sentence of the tenth paragraph?
28. What exactly is meant by "borrowing millions upon funds of interest"?
29. What bearing has the passage "People were tempted . . . with their money" (ll. 132–135) upon the preceding sentence?
30. What were "those new schemes of raising money"?
31. Substitute one word for the phrase "undertakers and projectors of loans and funds."
32. Give the derivation and meaning (in this extract) of faction, prerogative, monstrous, alliance, premiums, expedient, comply, contracted.
33. Learn by heart the fifth paragraph.
34. You may hold certain principles and keep silent; or you may hold them and, as long as you do not suffer, preach them; or you may hold them, and preach them, and suffer for them. With this train of thought in mind write a paragraph of which the first sentence is "During this struggle all thinking men began to consider what should be their attitude to warfare."

No. XVI

1. Most of my predecessors in this place have commended him who made this speech part of the law, telling us that it is well that it should be delivered at the burial

of those who fall in battle. For myself, I should have
5 thought that the worth which had displayed itself in deeds,
would be sufficiently rewarded by honors also shown by
deeds; such as you now see in this funeral prepared at the
people's cost. And I could have wished that the reputa-
tions of many brave men were not to be imperiled in the
10 mouth of a single individual, to stand or fall according
as he spoke well or ill. For it is hard to speak properly
upon a subject where it is even difficult to convince your
hearers that you are speaking the truth. On the one
hand, the friend who is familiar with every fact of the
15 story, may think that some point has not been set forth
with that fulness which he wishes and knows it to deserve;
on the other, he who is a stranger to the matter may be
led by envy to suspect exaggeration if he hears anything
above his own nature. For men can endure to hear others
20 praised only so long as they can severally persuade themselves of their own ability to equal the actions recounted:
when this point is passed, envy comes in and with it
incredulity. However, since our ancestors have stamped
this custom with their approval, it becomes my duty to
25 obey the law and to try to satisfy your several wishes and
opinions as best I may.

2. I shall begin with our ancestors: it is both just
and proper that they should have the honor of the first
mention on an occasion like the present. They dwelt in
30 the country without break in the succession from generation to generation, and handed it down free to the present
time by their valor. And if our more remote ancestors
deserve praise, much more do our own fathers, who added
to their inheritance the empire which we now possess,
35 and spared no pains to be able to leave their acquisitions
to us of the present generation. Lastly, there are few
parts of our dominions that have not been augmented
by those of us here, who are still more or less in the vigor
of life; while the mother country has been furnished by

us with everything that can enable her to depend on her 40
own resources whether for war or for peace. That part
of our history which tells of the military achievements
which gave us our several possessions, or of the ready
valor with which either we or our fathers stemmed the
tide of Hellenic or foreign aggression, is a theme too 45
familiar to my hearers for me to dilate on, and I shall
therefore pass it by. But what was the road by which
we reached our position, what the form of government
under which our greatness grew, what the national habits
out of which it sprang; these are questions which I may 50
try to solve before I proceed to my panegyric upon these
men; since I think this to be a subject upon which on the
present occasion a speaker may properly dwell, and to
which the whole assemblage, whether citizens or foreigners,
may listen with advantage.   55

3. Our Constitution does not copy the laws of neighboring states; we are rather a pattern to others than
imitators ourselves. Its administration favors the many
instead of the few; this is why it is called a democracy.
If we look to the laws, they afford equal justice to all in 60
their private differences; if to social standing, advancement in public life falls to reputation for capacity, class
considerations not being allowed to interfere with merit;
nor again does poverty bar the way; if a man is able to
serve the state, he is not hindered by the obscurity of 65
his condition. The freedom which we enjoy in our government extends also to our ordinary life. There, far from
exercising a jealous surveillance over each other, we do
not feel called upon to be angry with our neighbor for
doing what he likes, or even to indulge in those injurious 70
looks which cannot fail to be offensive, although they
inflict no positive penalty. But all this ease in our private
relations does not make us lawless as citizens. Against
this, fear is our chief safeguard, teaching us to obey the
magistrates and the laws, particularly such as regard the 75

protection of the injured, whether they are actually on the statute book, or belong to that code which, although unwritten, yet cannot be broken without acknowledged disgrace.

80   4. Further, we provide plenty of means for the mind to refresh itself from business. We celebrate games and sacrifices all the year round, and the elegance of our private establishments forms a daily source of pleasure and helps to banish the spleen; while the magnitude of our city draws
85 the produce of the world into our harbor, so that to the Athenian the fruits of other countries are as familiar a luxury as those of his own.

5. If we turn to our military policy, there also we differ from our antagonists. We throw open our city to the
90 world, and never by alien acts exclude foreigners from any opportunity of learning or observing, although the eyes of an enemy may occasionally profit by our liberality; trusting less in system and policy than to the native spirit of our citizens; while in education, where our rivals from
95 their very cradles by a painful discipline seek after manliness, at Athens we live exactly as we please, and yet are just as ready to encounter every legitimate danger. In proof of this it may be noticed that the Lacedæmonians do not invade our country alone, but bring with them all
100 their confederates; while we Athenians advance unsupported into the territory of a neighbor, and fighting upon a foreign soil usually vanquish with ease men who are defending their homes. Our united force was never yet encountered by any enemy, because we have at once
105 to attend to our marine and to despatch our citizens by land upon a hundred different services; so that, wherever they engage with some such fraction of our strength, a success against a detachment is magnified into a victory over the nation, and a defeat into a reverse suffered at the
110 hands of our entire people. And yet if with habits not of

labor but of ease, and courage not of art but of nature, we are still willing to encounter danger, we have the double advantage of escaping the experience of hardships in anticipation and of facing them in the hour of need as fearlessly as those who are never free from them. [115]

6. Nor are these the only points in which our city is worthy of admiration. We cultivate refinement without extravagance and knowledge without effeminacy; wealth we employ more for use than for show, and place the real [120] disgrace of poverty not in owning to the fact but in declining the struggle against it. Our public men have, besides politics, their private affairs to attend to, and our ordinary citizens, though occupied with the pursuits of industry, are still fair judges of public matters; for, [125] unlike any other nation, regarding him who takes no part in these duties not as unambitious but as useless, we Athenians are able to judge at all events if we cannot originate, and instead of looking on discussion as a stumbling-block in the way of action, we think it an [130] indispensable preliminary to any wise action at all. Again, in our enterprises we present the singular spectacle of daring and deliberation, each carried to its highest point, and both united in the same persons; although usually decision is the fruit of ignorance, hesitation of re- [135] flection. But the palm of courage will surely be adjudged most justly to those who best know the difference between hardship and pleasure and yet are never tempted to shrink from danger. In generosity we are equally singular, acquiring our friends by conferring not by [140] receiving favors. Yet, of course, the doer of the favor is the firmer friend of the two, in order by continued kind ness to keep the recipient in his debt; while the debtor feels less keenly from the very consciousness that the return he makes will be a payment, not a free gift. And [145] it is only the Athenians who, fearless of consequences,

confer their benefits not from calculations of expediency, but in the confidence of liberality.

7. In short, I say that as a city we are the school of
150 Hellas; while I doubt if the world can produce a man, who where he has only himself to depend upon, is equal to so many emergencies, and graced by so happy a versatility as the Athenian. And that this is no mere boast thrown out for the occasion, but plain matter of fact,
155 the power of the state acquired by these habits proves. For Athens alone of her contemporaries is found when tested to be greater than her reputation, and alone gives no occasion to her assailants to blush at the antagonist by whom they have been worsted, or to her subjects to
160 question her title by merit to rule. Rather, the admiration of the present and succeeding ages will be ours, since we have not left our power without witness, but have shown it by mighty proofs; and far from needing a Homer for our panegyrist, or other of his craft whose verses might
165 charm for the moment, only for the impression which they gave to melt at the touch of fact, we have forced every sea and land to be the highway of our daring, and everywhere, whether for evil or for good, have left imperishable monuments behind us. Such is the Athens
170 for which these men, in the assertion of their resolve not to lose her, nobly fought and died; and well may every one of their survivors be ready to suffer in her cause.

THUCYDIDES
(*Translated by Richard Crawley*)

QUESTIONS

1. Give a title to this extract.
2. Give titles to the paragraphs.

3. What is the purpose of the first two words in the second sentence of the first paragraph?

4. What is the purpose in its sentence of the phrase "to stand . . . well or ill" (l. 10)?

5. "In the first paragraph Pericles (who is speaking) argues that funeral panegyrics of this nature are . . . and . . ." Supply one word for each blank so that the completed sentence will summarize Pericles' attitude as indicated in the paragraph.

6. Give one phrase which will cover "our ancestors," "our own fathers," "those of us here." In order to do this study the first part of the second paragraph carefully and find out what characteristic was common to the actions of all.

7. What phrase in the second paragraph is recalled by the word "constitution" (l. 56)?

8. Write out three key-sentences of the third paragraph, which, put together, would present a just summary of the whole paragraph.

9. What was the test of merit among the Athenian citizens? Your answer can be given in a phrase of five words.

10. Somebody chose "means for the mind to refresh itself from business" as the key-phrase of the fourth paragraph. Criticize this. In order to do this you must study carefully every sentence in the paragraph.

11. What is the most significant phrase of the fifth paragraph? You must remember that you have to find a phrase that is relevant to the throwing open of the city to the world, as well as to the Athenian courage in the hour of need.

12. (a) What does Pericles mean by a "legitimate" danger (l. 97)?
    (b) What two phrases in the fifth paragraph may be brought into contrast with "legitimate danger"?

13. How was it that the Athenians escaped "the experience of hardships in anticipation"?

14. Can you suggest any reason why the cultivation of refinement might lead to extravagance, and the cultivation of knowledge to effeminacy?

15. Summarize in twelve words the passage "Our public men . . . wise action at all" (ll. 122–131).

16. (a) "We Athenians are able to judge . . . originate"
    (l. 127); in other words "the Athenians are . . .,
    if not . . ." Supply an adjective for each of the
    blanks.

    (b) "The Athenians are generous, not because they . . . but
    you because . . ." Fill in the blanks so as to show that
    you understand the phrases "calculations of expediency"
    and "confidence of liberality" (ll. 147–148).

17. Is there anything in the sixth paragraph that leads you to
    criticize Pericles' remark that Athenian generosity has
    nothing to do with expediency?

18. In what way does the last paragraph contribute to the
    whole extract?

19. "In short, I say that as a city we are the school of Hellas."
    Where else in this extract is much the same idea ex-
    pressed?

20. What is the key-sentence of the last paragraph?

21. Study the passage "and far from needing . . . monu-
    ments behind us" (ll. 163–169).

    (a) With what are the "imperishable monuments"
    contrasted?

    (b) What were those "imperishable monuments"?
    Answer the question by quoting from this para-
    graph a phrase of two words.

22. There are two instances in this extract of a faulty use of
    "while." What are these instances? What is faulty
    in them? Quote, from this extract, one legitimate use
    of "while."

23. Give the derivation and meaning (in this extract) of
    acquisitions, democracy, pattern, surveillance, delibera-
    tion, expediency, craft, charm, calculations.

24. Learn by heart the last paragraph of the extract.

25. "An empire is made by deeds not by words." Expand
    this thought into a paragraph. Think of some great
    English orators and of some great English men of action.
    Introduce references to them.

No. XVII

1. These excursions on foot or horseback formed by far
my most favorite amusement.   I have all my life delighted
in traveling, though I have never enjoyed that pleasure
upon a large scale.   It was a propensity which I sometimes
indulged so unduly as to alarm and vex my parents. 5
Wood, water, wilderness itself, had an inexpressible charm
for me, and I had a dreamy way of going much farther
than I intended, so that unconsciously my return was
protracted, and my parents had sometimes serious cause
of uneasiness.   For example, I once set out with Mr. 10
George Abercromby (the son of the immortal General),
Mr. William Clerk, and some others, to fish in the lake
above Howgate, and the stream which descends from it
into the Esk.   We breakfasted at Howgate, and fished
the whole day; and while we were on our return next 15
morning, I was easily seduced by William Clerk, then a
great intimate, to visit Pennycuik-House, the seat of his
family.   Here he and John Irving, and I for their sake,
were overwhelmed with kindness by the late Sir John
Clerk and his lady, the present Dowager Lady Clerk. 20
The pleasure of looking at fine pictures, the beauty of the
place, and the flattering hospitality of the owners, drowned
all recollection of home for a day or two.   Meanwhile our
companions, who had walked on without being aware of
our digression, returned to Edinburgh without us, and 25
excited no small alarm in my father's household.   At
length, however, they became accustomed to my escapades.
My father used to protest to me on such occasions that he
thought I was born to be a strolling peddler; and though
the prediction was intended to mortify my conceit, 30
I am not sure that I altogether disliked it.   I was now
familiar with Shakespeare, and thought of Autolycus's
song—

"Jog on, jog on, the footpath way,
    And merrily hent the stile-a;
A merry heart goes all the day,
    Your sad tires in a mile-a."

2. My principal object in these excursions was the
pleasure of seeing romantic scenery, or what afforded me
40 at least equal pleasure, the places which had been distinguished by remarkable historical events. The delight
with which I regarded the former, of course, had general
approbation, but I often found it difficult to procure
sympathy with the interest I felt in the latter. Yet to
45 me, the wandering over the field of Bannockburn was the
source of more exquisite pleasure than gazing upon the
celebrated landscape from the battlements of Stirling
Castle. I do not by any means infer that I was dead to the
feeling of picturesque scenery; on the contrary, few de-
50 lighted more in its general effect. But I was unable with
the eye of a painter to dissect the various parts of the
scene, to comprehend how the one bore upon the other,
to estimate the effect which various features of the view
had in producing its leading and general effect. I have
55 never, indeed, been capable of doing this with precision or
nicety, though my latter studies have led me to amend
and arrange my original ideas upon the subject. Even
the humble ambition, which I long cherished, of making
sketches of those places which interested me, from a
60 defect of eye or of hand was totally ineffectual. After long
study and many efforts, I was unable to apply the elements
of perspective or of shade to the scene before me, and was
obliged to relinquish in despair an art which I was most
anxious to practise. But show me an old castle or a field
65 of battle, and I was at home at once, filled it with its
combatants in their proper costume, and overwhelmed
my hearers by the enthusiasm of my description. In
crossing Magus Moor, near St. Andrews, the spirit moved
me to give a picture of the assassination of the Archbishop

of St. Andrews to some fellow-travelers with whom I was 70
accidentally associated, and one of them, though well
acquainted with the story, protested my narrative had
frightened away his night's sleep. I mention this to show
the distinction between a sense of the picturesque in action
and in scenery. If I have since been able in poetry to 75
trace with some success the principles of the latter, it has
always been with reference to its general and leading
features, or under some alliance with moral feeling; and
even this proficiency has cost me study. Meanwhile, I
endeavored to make amends for my ignorance of drawing 80
by adopting a sort of technical memory respecting the
scenes I visited. Wherever I went I cut a piece of a branch
from a tree—these constituted what I called my log-book;
and I intended to have a set of chessmen out of them,
each having reference to the place where it was cut—as 85
the kings from Falkland and Holy-Rood; the queens
from Queen Mary's yew tree at Crookston; the bishops
from abbeys or episcopal palaces; the knights from
baronial residences; the rooks from royal fortresses
and the pawns generally from places worthy of historical 90
note. But this whimsical design I never carried into
execution.

WALTER SCOTT

QUESTIONS

1. Give a title to this extract.
2. Give titles to the paragraphs.
3. What do you think is the key-sentence of the first paragraph? If you are tempted to choose the first sentence,
   think again.
4. What is the escapade related in the first paragraph an
   example of? "Scott's delight in traveling" is a poor
   answer, for it misses an essential point.
5. Why are the words, "without being aware of our digression"
   (l. 24) essential in their context?
6. Look up the word "litotes" in your dictionary. Can you

find an example in the first sentence of the second paragraph? If you can, justify your choice by quoting another instance from this paragraph, and one from the end of the first paragraph. Rewrite the sentences, keeping the same meaning, but getting rid of litotes.

7. What phrase in the second paragraph best indicates the scope of the paragraph?

8. Divide the second paragraph into five sections, *a, b, c, d, e,* and briefly indicate the scope of each section; thus

(*a*) "Scott's delight in romantic scenery and in places of historic interest, particularly the latter" ("My principal object . . . general effect.")

9. Supply one word for each of the following blanks: "Scott lacked the . . . knowledge of the painter; and was unable to appreciate the C . . . . n of a scene" (the dots represent letters).

10. Supply a phrase for the word "subject" (l. 57).

11. What does Scott mean by the "latter" (l. 76)?

12. Express as simply as you can in your own words Scott's meaning in the passage "If I have since . . . moral feeling" (ll. 75–78).

13. Substitute another adjective for "technical" (l. 81) which will show that you understand Scott's meaning.

14. Comment on the word "log-book" in this context (l. 83).

15. Which is the more common: a sense of the picturesque in action, or a sense of the picturesque in scenery? Justify your answer from this extract.

16. Summarize in 90–100 words the second paragraph as far as "cost me study" (l. 79).

17. Give the derivation and meaning (in this extract) of indulged, alarm, escapades, mortify, nicety, perspective, assassination, pawn, propensity, whimsical.

18. Learn by heart the passage: "But show me . . . and in scenery" (ll. 64–75).

19. You were expected home for dinner at one o'clock. But on the way something occurred of such interest that you stifled the pangs of hunger and did not return until the evening. Your description of what happened at home when you got back contains (among others) two consecutive paragraphs beginning as follows:

Paragraph A.   "And then, when father's breath gave out, I told him why I was late."

Paragraph B.   "But he was hardly mollified and told me that . . ."

Write paragraphs A. and B.   Note

(i) These are only two paragraphs from a much longer description.

(ii) For father you may substitute mother, uncle, aunt, or any other formidable relative.

No. XVIII

1. The Aspects of Nature, when considered from this point of view, are divisible into two classes: the first class being those which are most likely to excite the imagination; and the other class being those which address themselves to the understanding commonly so called, 5 that is, to the mere logical operations of the intellect. For although it is true that, in a complete and well-balanced mind, the imagination and the understanding each play their respective parts, and are auxiliary to each other, it is also true that, in a majority of instances, the 10 understanding is too weak to curb the imagination and restrain its dangerous licence.   The tendency of advancing civilization is to remedy this disproportion, and invest the reasoning powers with that authority which, in an early stage of society, the imagination exclusively possesses. 15 Whether or not there is ground for fearing that the reaction will eventually proceed too far, and that the reasoning faculties will in their turn tyrannize over the imaginative ones, is a question of the deepest interest; but, in the present condition of our knowledge, it is probably an 20 insoluble one.   At all events, it is certain that nothing like such a state has yet been seen; since, even in this age, when the imagination is more under control than in any preceding one, it has far too much power; as might be

25 easily proved, not only from the superstitions which in
every country still prevail among the vulgar, but also from
that poetic reverence for antiquity, which, though it has
been long diminishing, still hampers the independence,
blinds the judgment, and circumscribes the originality
30 of the educated classes.

2. Now, so far as natural phenomena are concerned, it is
evident, that whatever inspires feelings of terror, or of
great wonder, and whatever excites in the mind an idea of
the vague and uncontrollable, has a special tendency to
35 inflame the imagination, and bring under its dominion
the slower and more deliberate operations of the understanding. In such cases, Man, contrasting himself with
the force and majesty of Nature, becomes painfully con-
scious of his own insignificance. A sense of inferiority
40 steals over him. From every quarter innumerable
obstacles hem him in, and limit his individual will. His
mind, appalled by the indefined and indefinable, hardly
cares to scrutinize the details of which such imposing
grandeur consists. On the other hand, where the works
45 of Nature are small and feeble, Man regains confidence:
he seems more able to rely on his own power; he can,
as it were, pass through, and exercise authority in every
direction. And as the phenomena are more accessible,
it becomes easier for him to experiment on them, or to
50 observe them with minuteness; an inquisitive and analytic
spirit is encouraged, and he is tempted to generalize the
appearances of Nature, and refer them to the laws by which
they are governed.

3. Looking in this way at the human mind as affected
55 by the Aspects of Nature, it is surely a remarkable fact,
that all the great early civilizations were situated within
and immediately adjoining the tropics, where those aspects
are most sublime, most terrible, and where Nature is, in
every respect, most dangerous to Man. Indeed, generally,

in Asia, Africa, and America, the external world is more 60
formidable than in Europe. This holds good not only
of the fixed and permanent phenomena, such as mountains,
and other great natural barriers, but also of occasional
phenomena, such as earthquakes, tempests, hurricanes,
pestilences; all of which are in those regions very frequent, 65
and very disastrous. These constant and serious dangers
produce effects analogous to those caused by the sublimity
of Nature, in so far that in both cases there is a tendency
to increase the activity of the imagination. For the
peculiar province of the imagination being to deal with the 70
unknown, every event which is unexplained, as well as
important, is a direct stimulus to our imaginative faculties.
In the tropics, events of this kind are more numerous
than elsewhere; it therefore follows that in the tropics
the imagination is most likely to triumph. A few illustra- 75
tions of the working of this principle will place it in a
clearer light, and will prepare the reader for the arguments
based upon it.

4. Of those physical events which increase the insecurity
of Man, earthquakes are certainly among the most striking, 80
in regard to the loss of life which they cause, as also in
regard to their sudden and unexpected occurrence. There
is reason to believe that they are always preceded by atmospheric changes which strike immediately at the nervous
system, and thus have a direct physical tendency to impair 85
the intellectual powers. However this may be, there can
be no doubt as to the effect they produce in encouraging
particular associations and habits of thought. The terror
which they inspire, excites the imagination even to a painful extent, and, overbalancing the judgment, predisposes 90
men to superstitious fancies. And what is highly curious,
is, that repetition, so far from blunting such feelings,
strengthens them. In Peru, where earthquakes appear
to be more common than in any other country, every
succeeding visitation increases the general dismay; so that 95

in some cases, the fear becomes almost insupportable. The mind is thus constantly thrown into a timid and anxious state; and men witnessing the most serious dangers, which they can neither avoid nor understand, 100 become impressed with a conviction of their own inability, and of the poverty of their own resources. In exactly the same proportion, the imagination is aroused, and a belief in supernatural interference actively encouraged. Human power failing, superhuman power is called in; 105 the mysterious and the invisible are believed to be present; and there grow up among the people those feelings of awe, and of helplessness, on which all superstition is based, and without which no superstition can exist.

5. Further illustration of this may be found even in 110 Europe, where such phenomena are, comparatively speaking, extremely rare.   Earthquakes and volcanic eruptions are more frequent and more destructive in Italy, and in the Spanish and Portuguese peninsula, than in any other of the great countries; and it is precisely there that 115 superstition is most rife, and the superstitious classes most powerful.   Those were the countries where the clergy first established their authority, where the worst corruptions of Christianity took place, and where superstition has during the longest period retained the firmest hold. 120 To this may be added another circumstance, indicative of the connection between these physical phenomena and the predominance of the imagination.   Speaking generally, the fine arts are addressed more to the imagination; the sciences to the intellect.   Now it is remarkable, that all 125 the greatest painters, and nearly all the greatest sculptors, modern Europe has possessed, have been produced by the Italian and Spanish peninsulas.   In regard to science, Italy has no doubt had several men of conspicuous ability; but their numbers are out of all proportion small when 130 compared with her artists and poets.   As to Spain and Portugal, the literature of those two countries is eminently

poetic, and from their schools have proceeded some of the greatest painters the world has ever seen. On the other hand, the purely reasoning faculties have been neglected, and the whole peninsula, from the earliest 135 period to the present time, does not supply to the history of the natural sciences a single name of the highest merit, not one man whose works form an epoch in the progress of European knowledge.

HENRY THOMAS BUCKLE

QUESTIONS

1. Give a title to this extract.
2. Give titles to the paragraphs.
3. What sentence in the first paragraph most clearly indicates the scope of the paragraph?
4. Somebody, when asked to pick out the key-phrase of the first paragraph, selected "The Aspects of Nature." Criticize the choice.
5. Study the passage "the reasoning faculties will in their turn tyrannize over the imaginative ones." Now we may substitute for the phrase "such a state" (l. 22) another phrase indicating what that state is: viz. "such a . . . of the . . . over the . . ." Supply a word for each of the blanks. If you cannot do this, substitute some similar phrase of your own, beginning "such a . . ."
6. What, for the purposes of the argument in the first paragraph, is the essential characteristic common to the superstitions of the vulgar and a poetic reverence for antiquity?
7. Back to what sentence in the first paragraph does the first sentence in the second paragraph take us?
8. What operations of the understanding are indicated in the second paragraph?
9. Draw up in two columns the contrasting ideas of the second paragraph; thus—
   (a) Nature awe-inspiring, (a) Nature small and feeble. etc.

10. (a) Why is it remarkable that "all the great early civilizations" etc. (l. 56)?

    (b) Is there anything in the paragraph that justifies the word "remarkable"?

    (c) Quote a sentence from the *first* paragraph which also justifies the word.

11. What is the key-sentence of the third paragraph?

12. There are two aspects of nature mentioned in the third paragraph.

    (a) What are they?

    (b) What characteristics have they in common?

13. Summarize in twenty-five words the passage "For the peculiar province . . . triumph" (ll. 69–75).

14. "There is reason to believe" (l. 82). What phrase in the paragraph contrasts with this?

15. Reduce the fourth paragraph to a series of jottings; thus —"earthquakes—atmospheric changes influence the mind —certain habits of thought encouraged—superstitious fancies"—Now continue.

16. Why is it "highly curious" that repetition strengthens these fancies?

17. The passage "Human power . . . can exist" (ll. 104–108) consists of three sentences. In the first two sentences the normal construction of a sentence is followed—; viz. subject—predicate. But in the third this order is reversed—viz. predicate—subject. Why is this?

18. Substitute a phrase for "this" (l. 109), which will show clearly to what "this" refers.

19. The fourth and fifth paragraphs both illustrate the connection between physical phenomena and the predominance of the imagination. What is the difference between the two paragraphs?

20. Give the derivation and meaning (in this extract) of deliberate, disastrous, peculiar, superstition, volcanic, dismay (note particularly the derivation and comment upon it with reference to the context), phenomena, analytic, encouraged.

21. Learn by heart the second paragraph as far as "operations of the understanding."

22. Write a paragraph of which the following is the opening

and key-sentence: "But there are other works of
Nature which are, in comparison, small and feeble, and
upon which man is able to exert his intellect." In order
to do this you should consider what some of these works
of Nature are (*e.g.* rain, grassland, trees, etc.) and show
how man scrutinizes, experiments, classifies, and deduces
laws.   Do you know anything about science as applied
to agriculture?   What is meteorology?   (The last two
questions are merely thrown out in order to suggest lines
of thought and are not intended to be answered.   Other
questions will perhaps occur to you.)

No. XIX

1. From the first, his possession of a strong and brilliant
genius was acknowledged; and the extent of it seems
to have been guessed by others, before he was able to
persuade himself that he had claim to a place among the
masters of literature.   The ease with which he did every- 5
thing deceived him; and he probably would never have
done himself any measure of justice, even as compared
with those of his own time, but for the fact, which no
modesty could long veil, that whatever he did became
immediately "the fashion"—the object of all but universal 10
imitation.   Even as to this, he was often ready to surmise
that the priority of his own movement might have been
matter of accident; and certainly nothing can mark the
humility of his mind more strikingly than the style in
which he discusses, in his diary, the pretensions of the 15
pigmies that swarmed and fretted in the deep wake of his
mighty vessel.   To the really original writers among his
contemporaries he did full justice; no differences of
theory or taste had the least power to disturb his candor.
In some cases he rejoiced in feeling and expressing a cordial 20
admiration, where he was met by, at best, a cold and

grudging reciprocity: and in others, his generosity was
proof against not only the private belief but the public
exposure of envious malignity.   Lord Byron might well
25 say that Scott could be jealous of no one; but the im-
measurable distance did not prevent many from being
jealous of him.

2. His propensity to think too well of other men's works
sprung, of course, mainly from his modesty and good-
30 nature; but the brilliancy of his imagination greatly
sustained the delusion.   It unconsciously gave precision
to the trembling outline, and life and warmth to the vapid
colors before him.   This was especially the case as to
romances and novels; the scenes and characters in them
35 were invested with so much of the "light within," that he
would close with regret volumes which, perhaps, no other
person, except the diseased glutton of the circulating
library, ever could get half through.   Where colder critics
saw only a schoolboy's hollowed turnip with its inch of
40 tallow, he looked through the dazzling spray of his own
fancy, and sometimes the clumsy toy seems to have
swelled almost into "the majesty of buried Denmark."

3. These servile imitators are already forgotten, or will
soon be so; but it is to be hoped that the spirit which
45 breathes through his works may continue to act on our
literature, and consequently on the character and manners
of men.   The race that grew up under the influence of
that intellect can hardly be expected to appreciate fully
their own obligations to it: and yet if we consider what
50 were the tendencies of the minds and works that, but for
his, must have been unrivalled in the power and opportunity to mould young ideas, we may picture to ourselves
in some measure the magnitude of the debt we owe to a
perpetual succession, through thirty years, of publications
55 unapproached in charm, and all instilling a high and
healthy code; a bracing, invigorating spirit; a contempt

of mean passions, whether vindictive or voluptuous; humane charity, as distinct from moral laxity as from unsympathizing austerity; sagacity too deep for cynicism; and tenderness never degenerating into sentimentality: 60 animated throughout in thought, opinion, feeling, and style, by one and the same pure energetic principle—a pith and savor of manhood; appealing to whatever is good and loyal in our natures, and rebuking whatever is low and selfish. 65

JOHN GIBSON LOCKHART

QUESTIONS

1. Give a title to this extract.
2. Give titles to the paragraphs.
3. Divide the first paragraph into four sections *a, b, c, d,* and as briefly as possible indicate the scope of the sections; thus—
    (*a*) Scott's slowness to recognize his own genius.
      ("From the first . . . master of literature.")
4. In what way did "the ease with which he did everything" deceive Scott?
5. Explain the significance of the passage "even as compared with those of his own time" by filling in the blanks in the following: "Lockhart inserts the phrase 'even as compared with those of his own time' to show that Scott was not only . . . but also . . ." (More than one word for each blank will be required.)
6. What does Lockhart mean by "the priority . . . matter of accident" (ll. 12–13)?
7. (*a*) What is the full implication of "wake" (l. 16)?
    (*b*) Express quite simply the idea of the passage "the pretensions . . . vessel" by getting rid of the meta-phor.
8. "The outstanding characteristics of Scott's genius were . . . and . . ." Fill in the two blanks by two nouns taken from the first paragraph.
9. Study the passage "his generosity . . . malignity"

(ll. 22–24). Now express the idea in other words by filling in the blanks in the following: "Scott was generous in his attitude not only to those . . . but also to those . . ." (More than one word for each blank will be required.)

10. What are the two key-phrases of the second paragraph?

11. Give in not more than fifteen words the gist of the second paragraph.

12. Supply a conjunction to show the relationship between the two sentences "the brilliancy . . . delusion" and "It unconsciously . . . before him." (ll. 30–33.)

13. The idea which lies at the root of the word "invested" (l. 35) is that of clothing. Considering what some of the functions of clothing are, comment on the suitability of the word "invested" in this context.

14. What is the disease of the glutton in l. 37?

15. "'A schoolboy's hollowed turnip with its inch of tallow' is a metaphorical way of indicating a . . ." Supply a phrase for the blank.

16. You may, or may not, know that the words "the majesty of buried Denmark" refer to the ghost of Hamlet's murdered father. But, apart altogether from the allusion, what is the idea that Lockhart wishes to express?

17. In what way is the method of linking the second paragraph with the first similar to that of linking the third with the second?

18. What is the key-phrase of the third paragraph?

19. "Humane charity" (l. 58) may be defined as "compassionate lenience in judging others." What is the connection between humane charity and moral laxity? Between sagacity and cynicism? Between tenderness and sentimentality?

20. What word is qualified grammatically by "animated" (l. 61)?

21. "Loyal" (l. 64) means "faithful to." Faithful to what?

22. Learn by heart the passage "we may picture . . . low and selfish" (ll. 52-end).

23. Give the derivation and meaning (in this extract) of candor, reciprocity, generosity, propensity, precision, instil-

ling, austerity, cynicism (can you quote one example
of cynicism?), savor, rebuking, degenerating, code
(what has the tree-trunk got to do with it?).

24. Gummidge was a literary critic. Write two consecutive
paragraphs about him. The central idea of the first
paragraph is—his boasted ability to detect and expose
all the flaws in his contemporaries' works. The central
idea of the second paragraph is—his unhappy life and
miserable end.

No. XX

1. The method which Mr. Burke takes to prove that the
people of England have no such rights, and that such
rights do not now exist in the nation, either in whole or in
part, or anywhere at all, is of the same marvelous and
monstrous kind with what he has already said; for his 5
arguments are that the persons, or the generation of
persons, in whom they did exist, are dead, and with them
the right is dead also. To prove this, he quotes a declara-
tion made by Parliament about a hundred years ago,
to William and Mary, in these words: "The Lords 10
Spiritual and Temporal, and Commons, do, in the name of
the people aforesaid" (meaning the people of England
then living), "most humbly and faithfully *submit* themselves, their *heirs* and *posterities*, for EVER." He also
quotes a clause of another Act of Parliament made in the 15
same reign, the terms of which, he says, "bind us"
(meaning the people of that day), "our *heirs* and our
posterity, to *them*, their *heirs* and *posterity*, to the end of
time."

2. Mr. Burke conceives his point sufficiently established 20
by producing those clauses, which he enforces by saying
that they exclude the right of the nation for *ever*. And

not yet content with making such declarations, repeated
over and over again, he farther says, "that if the people
25 of England possessed such a right before the Revolution"
(which he acknowledges to have been the case, not only
in England, but throughout Europe, at an early period),
"yet that the *English nation* did, at the time of the
Revolution, most solemnly renounce and abdicate it,
30 for themselves, and for *all their posterity, for ever.*"

3. As Mr. Burke occasionally applies the poison drawn
from his horrid principles (if it is not profanation to call
them by the name of principles) not only to the English
nation, but to the French Revolution and the National
35 Assembly, and charges that august, illuminated, and illuminating body of men with the epithet of *usurpers*, I shall
sans cérémonie, place another system of principles in
opposition to his.

4. The English Parliament of 1688 did a certain thing,
40 which, for themselves and their constituents, they had a
right to do, and which it appeared right should be done:
but, in addition to this right, which they possessed by
delegation, *they set up another right by assumption*, that of
binding and controlling posterity to the end of time.
45 The case, therefore, divides itself into two parts: the right
which they possessed by delegation, and the right which
they set up by assumption.   The first is admitted; but
with respect to the second, I reply:

5. There never did, there never will, and there never
50 can, exist a Parliament, or any description of men, or any
generation of men, in any country, possessed of the right
or the power of binding and controlling posterity to the
"*end of time*," or of commanding for ever how the world
shall be governed, or who shall govern it; and, therefore,
55 all such clauses, acts, or declarations by which the makers
of them attempt to do what they have neither the right

nor the power to do, nor the power to execute, are in themselves null and void. Every age and generation must be as free to act for itself *in all cases* as the ages and generations which preceded it. The vanity and presump- tion of governing beyond the grave is the most ridiculous and insolent of all tyrannies. Man has no property in man; neither has any generation a property in the generations which are to follow. The Parliament or the people of 1688, or of any other period, had no more right to dispose of the people of the present day, or to bind, or to control them *in any shape whatever*, than the Parliament or the people of the present day have to dispose of, bind, or control those who are to live a hundred or a thousand years hence. Every generation is, and must be, competent to all the purposes which its occasions require. It is the living, and not the dead, that are to be accommodated. When man ceases to be, his power and his wants cease with him; and having no longer any participation in the concerns of this world, he has no longer any authority in directing who shall be its governors, or how its government shall be organized, or how administered.

6. I am not contending for nor against any form of government, nor for nor against any party, here or else- where. That which a whole nation chooses to do, it has a right to do. Mr. Burke says, No. Where, then, does the right exist? I am contending for the rights of the *living*, and against their being willed away, and controlled and contracted for, by the manuscript-assumed authority of the dead; and Mr. Burke is contending for the authority of the dead over the rights and freedom of the living. There was a time when kings disposed of their crowns by will upon their deathbeds, and consigned the people, like beasts of the field, to whatever successor they appointed. This is now so exploded as scarcely to be remembered, and so monstrous as hardly to be believed; but the Parliamentary clauses upon which

Mr. Burke builds his political church are of the same nature.

95   7. The laws of every country must be analogous to some common principle.   In England no parent or master, nor all the authority of Parliament, omnipotent as it has called itself, can bind or control the personal freedom even of an individual beyond the age of twenty-one years. 100 On what ground of right, then, could the Parliament of 1688, or any other Parliament, bind all posterity for ever?

8. Those who have quitted the world, and those who are not yet arrived at it, are as remote from each other as the utmost stretch of mortal imagination can conceive.   What 105 possible obligation, then, can exist between them; what rule or principle can be laid down that of two non-entities, the one out of existence and the other not in, and who never can meet in this world, the one should control the other to the end of time?

110   9. In England it is said that money cannot be taken out of the pockets of the people without their consent.   But who authorized, or who could authorize, the Parliament of 1688 to control and take away the freedom of posterity (who were not in existence to give or to withhold their 115 consent), and limit and confine their right of acting in certain cases for ever?

10. A greater absurdity cannot present itself to the understanding of man than what Mr. Burke offers to his readers.   He tells them, and he tells the world to come, 120 that a certain body of men who existed a hundred years ago, made a law, and that there does not now exist in the nation, nor ever will, nor ever can, a power to alter it. Under how many subtleties or absurdities has the divine right to govern been imposed on the credulity of mankind! 125 Mr. Burke has discovered a new one, and he has shortened

his journey to Rome by appealing to the power of this infallible Parliament of former days; and he produces what it has done as of divine authority, for that power must certainly be more than human which no human power to the end of time can alter.   130

THOMAS PAINE

QUESTIONS

1. Give a title to this extract.
2. Give titles to the paragraphs.
3. What are the rights to which Paine refers in l. 2?
4. What are Mr. Burke's "principles" (l. 32)?
5. The effect of poison is to kill or to injure a living organism. In what way do you suppose Paine thought that the principles, which you have just explained above, would kill or injure the English nation?
6. Give one sentence which explains Paine's principles. Look for it in the fifth paragraph.
7. What was the "certain thing" (l. 39)?
8. What was "this right" (l. 42)?
9. What is the difference between a right by delegation and a right by assumption?
10. What other words besides "delegation" and "assumption" are contrasted in the fourth paragraph?
11. What sentence in the fifth paragraph expresses the idea upon which Paine bases his whole argument?
12. Is there any difference in this context between "the power to do" and "the power to execute" (l. 57)? If so, try to explain why Paine inserts both.
13. What exactly does Paine mean by the vanity of governing beyond the grave?
14. What is the meaning of "Man has no property in man" (l. 62)? What is its connection with the preceding sentence?
15. (a) What do you think is the most controversial statement in the sixth paragraph?
    (b) Show that it *is* controversial.

16. Substitute for "political church" (l. 93) a noun to be found in the third paragraph.

17. In what way is it necessary to qualify the second sentence of the seventh paragraph?

18. What passage do you think gives the gist of the whole extract?

19. Explain the significance of "he has shortened his journey to Rome" (ll. 125–126).

20. Do *you* believe that there is any "possible obligation" that can exist between the living and the dead?

21. "He was so badly wounded that he could not have crawled five yards; therefore he could not have run half a mile." This is an *a fortiori* argument.   Look up *a fortiori* in your dictionary and quote two examples from this extract. On what does the validity of this type of argument depend?

22. Give the derivation and meaning (in this extract) of monstrous, profanation, august, constituents, accommodated, obligation, principles.

23. Learn by heart the eighth paragraph.

24. Summarize the whole extract in 40–50 words.

25. In order to commemorate his long association with the public life of his city, a certain gentleman, at death, left a sum of money for the erection and maintenance of a public fountain in one of the main streets.   The city authorities accepted the gift and the fountain was duly erected.   Nearly a century later, however, owing to the growth of population and consequent development in building and road-construction, this fountain came to be regarded by the more progressive party in the Town Council as something of a nuisance, and proposals were put forward for its demolition.   The more conservative party opposed this suggestion on the grounds that, since it had been accepted by their predecessors as a gift, and, moreover, was maintained by funds from the same bequest, the Council had no right to order its destruction.   Write a letter to your local paper giving your views on the question.

No. XXI

1. In hope of giving longevity to that which its own nature forbids to be immortal, I have devoted this book, the labor of years, to the honor of my country, that we may no longer yield the palm of philology, without a contest, to the nations of the continent. The chief glory 5 of every people arises from its authors; whether I shall add anything by my own writings to the reputation of English literature must be left to time: much of my life has been lost under the pressure of disease; much has been trifled away; and much has always been spent in 10 provision for the day that was passing over me; but I shall not think my employment useless or ignoble, if by my assistance foreign nations, and distant ages, gain access to the propagators of knowledge, and understand the teachers of truth; if my labors afford light to the 15 repositories of science, and add celebrity to Bacon, to Hooker, to Milton, and to Boyle.

2. When I am animated by this wish, I look with pleasure on my book, however defective, and deliver it to the world with the spirit of a man that has endeavored well. That 20 it will immediately become popular I have not promised to myself; a few wild blunders, and risible absurdities, from which no work of much multiplicity was ever free, may for a time furnish folly with laughter, and harden ignorance in contempt; but useful diligence will at last 25 prevail, and there can never be wanting some who distinguish desert, who will consider that no dictionary of a living tongue can ever be perfect, since, while it is hastening to publication, some words are budding, and some falling away; that a whole life cannot be spent upon syntax 30 and etymology, and that even a whole life would not be sufficient; that he whose design includes whatever language can express, must often speak of what he does not

understand; that a writer will sometimes be hurried by
35 eagerness to the end, and sometimes faint with weariness
under a task which Scaliger compares to the labors of the
anvil and the mine; that what is obvious is not always
known, and what is known is not always present; that
sudden fits of inadvertency will surprise vigilance, slight
40 avocations will seduce attention, and casual eclipses of
the mind will darken learning; and that the writer shall
often in vain trace his memory, at the moment of need,
for that which yesterday he knew with intuitive readiness,
and which will come uncalled into his thoughts tomorrow.
45 In this work, when it shall be found that much is omitted,
let it not be forgotten that much likewise is performed;
and though no book was ever spared out of tenderness to
the author, and the world is little solicitous to know
whence proceeded the faults of that which it condemns,
50 yet it may gratify curiosity to inform it that the *English
Dictionary* was written with little assistance of the learned,
and without any patronage of the great; not in the soft
obscurities of retirement, or under the shelter of academic
bowers, but amid inconvenience and distraction, in sickness
55 and in sorrow.   It may repress the triumph of malignant
criticism to observe that if our own language is not here
fully displayed, I have only failed in an attempt which
no human powers have hitherto completed.   If the lexicons
of ancient tongues, now immutably fixed, and comprised
60 in a few volumes, be yet, after the toil of successive ages,
inadequate and delusive, if the aggregated knowledge
and coöperating diligence of the Italian academicians
did not secure them from the censure of Beni; if the
embodied critics of France, when fifty years had been
65 spent upon their work, were obliged to change its economy,
and give their second edition another form, I may surely
be contented without the praise of perfection, which, if I
could obtain, in this gloom of solitude, what would it avail
me?   I have protracted my work till most of those whom
70 I wished to please have sunk into the grave, and success

and miscarriage are empty sounds; I therefore dismiss it with frigid tranquillity, having little to fear or hope from censure or from praise.

SAMUEL JOHNSON

QUESTIONS

1. Give a title to this extract.
2. Give titles to the paragraphs.
3. (a) With what is "longevity" contrasted in the first sentence?
   (b) What is "that which" (l. 1)?
   (c) Why does its own nature forbid it to be immortal?
4. In the second sentence of the first paragraph there are a phrase and a word which carry us back in thought to a phrase and a word in the first sentence. What are the two phrases and the two words?
5. What does Johnson mean by "provision for the day that was passing over me" (l. 11)?
6. (a) In what way does the second sentence of the first paragraph differ from all the other sentences of the paragraph?
   (b) What is the relation in thought between this second sentence and the one that precedes it?
7. Write out the key-sentence of the second paragraph. You will find that this sentence looks both backwards and forwards.
8. "This wish" (l. 18). What wish? Answer in a phrase of three words.
9. How does contempt harden ignorance?
10. Why is laughter so often the expression of folly? The derivation of "folly" should help you to an answer.
11. What fact about language does Johnson seek to emphasize by using the phrase "*hastening* to publication" (l. 28), instead of using some such phrase as "being prepared for publication"?
12. Summarize in ten phrases the ten reasons given by Johnson why "no dictionary of a living tongue can ever be perfect." You might start thus:

(1) The continuous process of change in language.

(2) The limitations of time.

You may think that there are eleven reasons; show that your No. 11 may be regarded as an elaborated version of No. 7.

13. Compare the first and last sentences of the second paragraph.   What thoughts are suggested by the comparison?

14. Why did Scaliger compare the task of a lexicographer to the "labors of the anvil and the mine"?   You should consider very carefully the significance of the anvil and the mine in this context.

15. Why is "darken" (l. 41) an appropriate word in this context?

16. With what is the aggregated knowledge and coöperating diligence of the Italian academicians contrasted?

17. What does Johnson mean by "who distinguished desert," "academic bowers," "immutably fixed," "aggregated knowledge," "embodied critics"?

18. "The writer shall often trace . . . his thoughts to-morrow" (ll. 41–44).   The above sentence illustrates "the . . . of memory."   Supply one word for the blank.

19. What figure of speech is illustrated in the last sentence of the extract?   Carefully define that figure of speech.

20. Give the derivation and meaning (in this extract) of longevity, propagators, repositories, risible, syntax, etymology, inadvertency, avocations, intuitive, solicitous, economy, popular.

21. Summarize in twenty-five words the passage: "That it will immediately become popular . . . his thoughts tomorrow" (ll. 20–44).

22. Learn by heart the two passages

    (a) "The chief glory . . . Boyle" (ll. 5–17).

    (b) "I have protracted . . . praise" (ll. 69-end).

23. You were given an essay to write.   You dreaded the task. Contrary to your expectations it turned out a great success.   Write two paragraphs.   The first begins: "The subject, I felt, was quite beyond me"; and the second begins: "And courage had its reward."

    The first part of your first paragraph should mention some general reasons why everybody found it hard to write on this particular subject, which, by the way, you should specify. The second part of the first paragraph should mention some reasons peculiar to yourself (*e.g.* you were ill; or, you were absent from school when the subject was dealt with; or, you had no access to a library; or, certain circumstances in your life made the subject distasteful to you, etc., etc.). In writing the last sentence of this paragraph keep in mind the first sentence of the following paragraph.

The second paragraph should show how your difficulties melted away, and you should be continually returning in thought to the first paragraph.

No. XXII

1. I have said that all branches of knowledge are connected together, because the subject-matter of knowledge is intimately united in itself, as being the great Creator and His work. Hence it is that the sciences, into which our knowledge may be said to be cast, have multiplied bearings 5 one on another, and an internal sympathy, and admit, or rather demand, comparison and adjustment. They complete, correct, balance each other. This consideration, if well-founded, must be taken into account, not only as regards the attainment of truth, which is their common 10 end, but as regards the influence which they exercise upon those whose education consists in the study of them. I have said already, that to give undue prominence to one is to be unjust to another; to neglect or supersede these is to divert those from their proper object. It is to unsettle 15 the boundary lines between science and science, to disturb their action, to destroy the harmony which binds them together. Such a proceeding will have a corresponding effect when introduced into a place of education. There is no science but tells a different tale, when viewed 20

as a portion of a whole, from what it is likely to suggest when taken by itself, without the safeguard, as I may call it, of others.

2. Let me make use of an illustration. In the combination of colors, very different effects are produced by a difference in their selection and juxtaposition; red, green, and white change their shades, according to the contrast to which they are submitted. And, in like manner, the drift and meaning of a branch of knowledge varies with the company in which it is introduced to the student. If his reading is confined simply to one subject, however such division of labor may favor the advancement of a particular pursuit, a point into which I do not here enter, certainly it has a tendency to contract his mind. If it is incorporated with others, it depends on those others as to the kind of influence which it exerts upon him. Thus, the Classics, which in England are the means of refining the taste, have in France subserved the spread of revolutionary and deistical doctrines. In metaphysics, again, Butler's *Analogy of Religion*, which has had so much to do with the conversion of members of the University of Oxford, appeared to Pitt and others, who had received a different training, to operate only in the direction of infidelity. And so again, Watson, Bishop of Llandaff, as I think he tells us in the narrative of his life, felt the science of mathematics to indispose the mind to religious belief, while others see in its investigations the best defence of the Christian Mysteries. In like manner, I suppose, Arcesilas would not have handled logic as Aristotle, nor Aristotle have criticized poets as Plato; yet reasoning and poetry are subject to scientific rules.

3. It is a great point then to enlarge the range of studies which a university professes, even for the sake of the students; and, though they cannot pursue every subject which is open to them, they will be the gainers by living among those and under those who represent the whole

circle.   This I conceive to be the advantage of a seat of universal learning, considered as a place of education. An assemblage of learned men, zealous for their own sciences, and rivals of each other, are brought, by familiar intercourse and for the sake of intellectual peace, to adjust together the claims and relations of their respective subjects of investigation.   They learn to respect, to consult, to aid each other.   Thus is created a pure and clear atmosphere of thought, which the student also breathes, though in his own case he only pursues a few sciences out of the multitude.   He profits by an intellectual tradition, which is independent of particular teachers, which guides him in his choice of subjects, and duly interprets for him those which he chooses.   He apprehends the great outlines of knowledge, the principles on which it rests, the scale of its parts, its lights and its shades, its great points and its little, as he otherwise cannot apprehend them.   Hence it is that his education is called "Liberal."   A habit of mind is formed which lasts through life, of which the attributes are, freedom, equitableness, calmness, moderation, and wisdom; or what in a former Discourse I have ventured to call a philosophical habit.   This then I would assign as the special fruit of the education furnished at a university, as contrasted with other places of teaching or modes of teaching.   This is the main purpose of a university in its treatment of its students.

JOHN HENRY NEWMAN[1]

QUESTIONS

1. Give a title to this extract.
2. Give titles to the paragraphs.
3. What is the key-sentence of the first paragraph?
4. What is "the subject-matter of knowledge" (l. 2)?
5. What is the difference between the sciences and knowledge?
6. What is the relation in thought between "they complete,

---

[1]Reprinted from *University Education* by permission of Longmans, Green & Co., Ltd., London.

correct, balance each other" and the preceding passage beginning with "Hence . . ."?   (ll. 4–8.)

7. "their common end" (l. 10).   The common end of what?

8. What is the relation of the sentence "red, green, and white . . . submitted" (ll. 26–28) to the preceding sentence?

9. Show from a consideration of your own school time-table how the various subjects of study complete and correct each other. Could you, for example, drop geography without in any way impairing your study of history? No detailed discussion is asked for here. All that is necessary is a sentence or two to show that you do understand how one branch of knowledge can affect another.

10. What truth do the illustrations given in the passage "Thus the Classics . . . scientific rules" (ll. 36–51) seek to impress?

11. What is the force of the last sentence of the second paragraph so far as Newman's argument is concerned? It may help you to an answer if you consider whether there is anything else that affects reasoning and poetry besides scientific rules.

12. "Even for the sake of the students" (l. 53).   For what other purpose might they be enlarged?

13. If you study the last paragraph carefully you should be able to divide the members of a university into two classes. What are they? If you can, use words taken from the paragraph.

14. What do you consider to be the key-phrase of the last paragraph?

15. Summarize the last paragraph in thirty words.

16. "Considered as a place of education." How else might a university be considered?

17. The last paragraph may be divided into two parts, A and B, of which B is an amplification of A. Show where the division occurs.

18. (a) What "other places of teaching" can you mention where the education received would not be considered "liberal"?

    (b) In what respects do they differ from a university?

19. Learn by heart the passage "He profits by an intellectual tradition . . . moderation and wisdom" (ll. 67–77).

20. Give the derivation and meaning (in this extract) of science, education, incorporated, metaphysics, investigations, university, liberal.

21. Is a Debating Society a place where a pure and clear atmosphere of thought is created? Answer the question in a carefully written paragraph.

No. XXIII

1. Man's imagination is limited by the horizon of his experience. When he attempts by guess-work to outgo the bounds assigned, his frailty and ignorance stand apparent; he is like a child explaining the world by its doll's-house. The irremovable boundaries of knowledge are the same 5 for every age; human sense is feeble, human reason whimsical and vain, human life short and troubled. But every now and then, in the long history of the race, there is a rift in the cloud, or a new prospect gained by climbing. These are the great ages of the world. Creation widens 10 on the view, and the air is alive with a sense of promise and expectancy. Thus it was in the age of Elizabeth. The recovery of the Classics opened a long and fair vista backwards; the exploration of the New World seemed to lift the curtain on a glorious future. And the English, 15 the little parochial people, who for centuries had tilled their fields and tended their cattle in their island home, cut off from the great movements of European policy, suddenly found themselves, by virtue of their shipping, competitors for the dominion of the earth. It is no wonder 20 that their hearts distended with pride, and, hardening in their strength, gloried. A new sense of exaltation possessed the country, the exaltation of knowledge and power. The rising tide of national enthusiasm flooded the literature of the people, and surprised the dwellers on many a high 25 and dry inland creek.

2. Charles Lamb, who loved all that is familiar and ancient and homely, somewhere expresses regret that the

plays of Shakespeare and some of his brother dramatists
30 hardly ever choose as their theme the simple daily life of
the England of their own time, the affairs of the shopkeepers of Cheapside, or of the countrymen of Essex.   Had
the dramatists been of his mind, we should have had no
great English drama, and no Shakespeare.   The regret
35 felt by Lamb is only natural; he was a true antiquary,
and the touch of antiquity has gilded the bucolics and
citizens of Shakespeare's time.   Vulgarity and stupidity
are amiable enough in dead men.   But the question at
issue was a live question in the time of Elizabeth.   The
40 men of the new school turned impatiently away from the
self-satisfied insularity and rustic ineptitude of their
forbears, and hastened to become citizens of the world.
The infection of foreign literatures and foreign travel
changed customs and manners so fast that many sober
45 observers stood aghast at the rapidity of the movement,
and the country rang with denunciations of the innovators.
In a single generation the change was complete.   At the
time of Hawkins' earlier voyages *Gammer Gurton's Needle*
was a comedy of the newest fashion, and the highest reach
50 of English tragedy was still to be sought in the Miracle-
plays; before he died *Love's Labor's Lost* and *Doctor
Faustus* had been seen on the boards of the London theaters.
Action and imagination went hand in hand.   If the
voyagers explored new countries, and trafficked with strange
55 peoples, the poets and dramatists went abroad too, and
rifled foreign nations, returning with far-fetched and dear-
bought wares; or explored lonely and untried recesses of
the microcosm of man.   One spirit of discovery and
exultant power animated both seamen and poets.   Shake-
60 speare and Marlowe were, no less than Drake and Caven-
dish, circumnavigators of the world.

WALTER RALEIGH (1861–1922)[1]

---

[1]Reprinted from *The English Voyages of the Sixteenth Century* by permission
of Jackson, Wylie & Co., London.

1. Give a title to this extract.
2. Give titles to the paragraphs.
3. The first paragraph may be divided into two sections—
    (a) General statement of a truth.
    (b) A special instance of this truth.
    Indicate the sections.
4. With what is "guess-work" contrasted (l. 2)? horizon of this experience
5. What is it that "the child" (l. 4) lacks? experience of the world
6. Study the passage "the irremovable boundaries . . . and troubled" (ll. 5–7). Now substitute another word for "experience" (l. 2).
7. What determines the boundaries of knowledge?
8. Mention four words in the passage "But every now and then . . . expectancy" (ll. 7–12) that take us back in thought to the word "horizon" (l. 1).
9. The sense of the above passage (No. 8) may be summarized thus, "The great ages of the world are those in which man's knowledge is stimulated by a sudden increase of his imagination." Supply one word for each blank.
10. The Elizabethan gained a new prospect by "climbing." What phrases in section (b) (see No. 3 above) correspond to climbing?
11. Why does Sir Walter Raleigh insert the passage "the little parochial people . . . policy" (ll. 16–18)? to contrast - with
12. Consider the meaning of "exaltation" (l. 22). Back to what word in the first section of the paragraph does it take us?
13. Write down four key-words which indicate the effect upon the minds of the Elizabethans of their widening horizon.
14. The last two sentences of the first paragraph both assert the prevalence of a new spirit in Elizabethan England. But there is an important difference between the two sentences. What is it? Show that the difference is important with reference to the next paragraph. What is the word in the last sentence that prepares us for the next paragraph?
15. The idea of the last sentence of the first paragraph might be expressed thus: "This national enthusiasm influenced

Elizabethan literature even in . . ." Complete the sentence in such a way as will show that you understand the meaning of the phrase "the dwellers on many a high and dry inland creek."

16. What do you consider to be the key-sentence of the first paragraph?

17. Divide the second paragraph into the following sections—
    (a) Charles Lamb's wish not . . . with great English drama.
    (b) Reason for (a).
    (c)   . . .
    (d)   . . .
    Fill with an adjective the blank in (a), supply titles for (c) and (d), and show where the divisions occur.

18. In what way does the phrase "the affairs of the shopkeepers . . . Essex" contribute to the sentence in which it occurs?

19. What is the connection in thought between the passage "he was a true antiquary . . . Shakespeare's time" (ll. 35–37) and the preceding sentence?

20. Consider the sentence "the touch of antiquity . . . Shakespeare's time." The idea may be expressed thus: "The bucolics and citizens of Shakespeare's time, separated from us by over three centuries, appear . . ." Complete the sentence to show that you understand Sir Walter Raleigh's meaning. More than one word, of course, is required. Avoid metaphors.

21. Where else in the paragraph is the idea of "bucolics and citizens" expressed?

22. Charles Lamb loved "all that is familiar and ancient and homely." "Vulgarity and stupidity are amiable enough in dead men." Did Lamb love all that was vulgar and stupid?

23. What was the essential difference between Lamb's attitude to the simple daily life of Elizabethan England, and Shakespeare's? Work into your answer a sentence taken from this paragraph.

24. What idea in the passage "The men of the new school . . . world" is most prominently elaborated in the following sentence?

25. What word in the second paragraph indicates the same idea as "the men of the new school"?

26. To what divisions of drama do *Love's Labor's Lost* and *Doctor Faustus* respectively belong? You may already know. But if you do not, the answer will be suggested by a careful study of the context.

27. An idea may be developed
    (a) by proceeding from the particular to the general, *e.g.* "For this gallant action he was awarded the V.C. Courage generally has its reward"; or
    (b) by proceeding from the general to the particular, *e.g.* "The invention of a new weapon in warfare always arouses protest. There was a great outcry in Europe when the broadsword was superseded by the rapier, and a tall man of his hands could be spitted like a cat or a rabbit by any dexterous little fellow with a trained wrist."

    In the second paragraph quote a passage corresponding to (a), and one corresponding to (b).

28. (A difficult question unless you know something about Elizabethan drama)—Can you justify the epithet "dear-bought" (l. 56)?

29. What is meant by "explored lonely and untried recesses of the microcosm of man" (l. 57)?

30. What do you consider the key-sentence of the second paragraph?

31. Give the derivation and meaning (in this extract) of horizon, parochial, vulgarity, enthusiasm, ineptitude, microcosm.

32. Learn by heart the passage "And the English . . . creek" (ll. 15–26).

33. Think of what goes to make a great nation. The annalist is the mere recorder of events. The poet is sensitive to catch the spirit animating those events. If you can, read Julian Grenfell's *Into Battle;* it is not a mere narration of what happened; it interprets the spirit of the finest type of fighting man.

    With this train of thought in mind, write a paragraph of which the following is the opening and key-sentence: "A nation must have its poets as well as its annalists."

No. XXIV

1. It is true, all things have two faces, a light one and
a dark.   It is true, in three centuries much imperfection
accumulates; many an Ideal, monastic or other, shooting
forth into practice as it can, grows to a strange enough
5 Reality; and we have to ask with amazement, Is this
your Ideal!   For, alas, the Ideal always has to grow in
the Real, and to seek out its bed and board there, often
in a very sorry way.   No beautifulest Poet is a Bird-of-
Paradise, living on perfumes; sleeping in the æther with
10 outspread wings.   The Heroic, *independent* of bed and
board, is found in Drury-Lane Theater only; to avoid
disappointments, let us bear this in mind.

2. By the law of Nature, too, all manner of Ideals have
their fatal limits and lot; their appointed periods, of youth,
15 of maturity or perfection, of decline, degradation, and
final death and disappearance.   There is nothing born but
has to die.   Ideal monasteries, once grown real, do seek
bed and board in this world; do find it more and more
successfully; do get at length too intent on finding it,
20 exclusively intent on that.   They are then like diseased
corpulent bodies fallen idiotic, which merely eat and sleep;
ready for "dissolution," by a Henry the Eighth or some
other.   Jocelin's St. Edmundsbury is still far from this
last dreadful state: but here, too, the reader will prepare
25 himself to see an Ideal not sleeping in the æther like a
bird-of-paradise, but roosting as the common wood-fowl do,
in an imperfect, uncomfortable, more or less contemptible
manner!

3. Abbot Hugo, as Jocelin, breaking at once into the
30 heart of the business, apprises us, had in those days grown
old, grown rather blind, and his eyes were somewhat
darkened, *aliquantulum caligaverunt oculi ejus.*   He dwelt

apart very much, in his *Talamus* or peculiar Chamber;
got into the hands of flatterers, a set of mealy-mouthed
persons who strove to make the passing hour easy for him 35
—for him easy, and for themselves profitable; accumu-
lating in the distance mere mountains of confusion. Old
Dominus Hugo sat inaccessible in this way, far in the
interior, wrapped in his warm flannels and delusions;
inaccessible to all voice of Fact; and bad grew ever worse 40
with us. Not that our worthy old *Dominus Abbas* was
inattentive to the divine offices, or to the maintenance
of a devout spirit in us or in himself; but the Account-
Books of the Convent fell into the frightfulest state, and
Hugo's annual Budget grew yearly emptier, or filled with 45
futile expectations, fatal deficit, wind, and debts!

4. His one worldly care was to raise ready money;
sufficient for the day is the evil thereof. And how he
raised it: From usurious insatiable Jews; every fresh
Jew sticking on him like a fresh horse-leech, sucking his 50
and our life out; crying continually, Give, give! Take
one example instead of scores. Our *Camera*[1] having fallen
into ruin, William the Sacristan received charge to repair
it; strict charge, but no money; Abbot Hugo would, and
indeed could, give him no fraction of money. The Camera 55
in ruins, and Hugo penniless and inaccessible. Willelmus
Sacrista borrowed Forty Marks (some seven-and-twenty
pounds) of Benedict the Jew, and patched up our Camera
again. But the means of repaying him? There were no
means. Hardly could Sacrista, Cellerarius, or any public 60
officer, get ends to meet, on the indispensablest scale, with
their shrunk allowances: ready money had vanished.

5. Benedict's Twenty-seven pounds grew rapidly at compound interest; and at length, when it had amounted to a
Hundred pounds, he, on a day of settlement, presents the 65
account to Hugo himself. Hugo already owed him another

---

[1] *I.e.,* Abbot's House.

hundred of his own; and so here it has become **Two**
Hundred! Hugo, in a fine frenzy, threatens to depose **the**
Sacristan, to do this and do that; but, in the meanwhile,
70 how to quiet your insatiable Jew? Hugo, for this couple
of hundreds, grants the Jew his bond for Four Hundred
payable at the end of four years. At the end of four years
there is, of course, still no money; and the Jew now gets
a bond for Eight hundred and eighty pounds, to be paid
75 by instalments, Fourscore pounds every year. Here was
a way of doing business!

6. Neither yet is this insatiable Jew satisfied or settled
with: he had papers against us of "small debts fourteen
years old"; his modest claim amounts finally to "Twelve
80 hundred pounds besides interest";—and one hopes he
never got satisfied in this world; one almost hopes he was
one of those beleaguered Jews who hanged themselves in
York Castle shortly afterwards, and had his usances and
quittances and horse-leech papers summarily set fire to!
85 For approximate justice will strive to accomplish itself;
if not in one way, then in another. Jews, and also Chris-
tians and Heathens, who accumulate in this manner,
though furnished with never so many parchments, do,
at times, "get their grinder-teeth successively pulled out
90 of their head, each day a new grinder," till they consent to
disgorge again. A sad fact,—worth reflecting on.

7. Jocelin, we see, is not without secularity: **Our**
Dominus Abbas was intent enough on the divine offices;
but then his Account-books—?—. One of the things that
95 strike us most, throughout, in Jocelin's *Chronicle*, and indeed in Eadmer's *Anselm*, and other old monastic books,
written evidently by pious men, is this: That there is
almost no mention whatever of "personal religion" in
them; that the whole gist of their thinking and speculation
100 seems to be the "privileges of our order," "strict exaction
of our dues," "God's honor" (meaning the honor of

our Saint), and so forth.   Is not this singular?   A body of men, set apart for perfecting and purifying their own souls, do not seem disturbed about that in any measure: the "Ideal" says nothing about its idea; says much about finding bed and board for itself!   How is this? 105

8. Why, for one thing, bed and board are a matter very apt to come to speech: it is much easier to *speak* of them than of ideas; and they are sometimes much more pressing with some!   Nay, for another thing, may not this religious reticence, in these devout, good souls, be 110 perhaps a merit, and sign of health in them?   Jocelin, Eadmer, and such religious men, have as yet nothing of "Methodism"; no Doubt or even root of Doubt.   Religion is not a diseased self-introspection, an agonizing 115 inquiry: their duties are clear to them, the way of supreme good plain, indisputable, and they are traveling on it. Religion lies over them like an all-embracing heavenly canopy, like an atmosphere and life-element, which is not spoken of, which in all things is pre-supposed without 120 speech.   Is not serene or complete Religion the highest aspect of human nature; as serene Cant, or complete No-religion, is the lowest and miserablest?   Between which two, all manner of earnest Methodisms, introspections, agonizing inquiries, never so morbid, shall play their respec- 125 tive parts, not without approbation.

THOMAS CARLYLE

QUESTIONS

1. Give a title to this extract.
2. Give titles to the paragraphs.
3. What is the key-sentence of the first paragraph?
4. Give one verb for "seek out its bed and board."
5. What is there about "a Bird-of-Paradise living on

fumes, sleeping in the æther with outspread wings" that makes it suitable for Carlyle's argument in the first paragraph?

6. What is the relation between the passage "No beautifulest poet . . . bear in mind" (ll. 8–12) and the sentence immediately preceding?

7. Why is it that a theatrical performance can present the Heroic "independent of bed and board"?

8. Rearrange the second paragraph thus:
   (a) General statement of a truth.
   (b) A special instance of this truth.
   (c) A special instance of (b).
   (d) A special instance of (c).
   Show where these sections begin and end.

9. Why are the limits "fatal" (l. 14)?

10. Why is "dissolution" put between inverted commas?

11. What for the purposes of this extract was the most important of Abbot Hugo's delusions?

12. Is there anything in the third paragraph that recalls the Ideal?

13. "Abbot Hugo was . . ." Complete this by means of a phrase so that your sentence will show that you understand the significance of "sufficient for the day is the evil thereof."

14. Can you find a phrase in the third paragraph which is recalled by "sufficient for the day is the evil thereof"?

15. Summarize in fifty words the passage "His one worldly care . . . Here was a way of doing business" (ll. 47–76).

16. (a) What does Carlyle mean by "approximate" justice?
    (b) Is there any other word in the paragraph which shows that the justice was approximate?

17. What was the monastic ideal as set out in the seventh paragraph?

18. "In the seventh paragraph Carlyle marvels at the . . . of the monastic . . ." Supply one word for each blank.

19. What is the relation between the two passages "one of the things . . . singular" (ll. 94–102), and "A body of men . . . How is this?" (ll. 102–106)?

20. What phrase in the eighth paragraph might be taken as indicating the scope of the preceding paragraph?

21. What relation has the eighth paragraph to the seventh?

22. Study the phrase "an agonizing inquiry" (l. 115). Inquiry into what? What sentence in the paragraph suggests an answer?

23. What is there in common between an atmosphere and the religion of these old monks?

24. What was the distinguishing characteristic of the monks' religion as indicated in the last paragraph of the extract?

25. What two words in the last paragraph pick up by way of contrast the idea contained in the word "health" (l. 112)?

26. Give the derivation and meaning (in this extract) of ideal (note very carefully its derivation), exclusively, usurious, cant, insatiable, gist, secularity, idiotic, privileges, reticence, respective (is the word necessary in this context? Write a sentence in which "respective" is undoubtedly necessary).

27. "She washed with happiness and Pears' soap." This is an example of the rhetorical figure known as *syllepsis*. Without consulting your dictionary, write a definition of *syllepsis* and quote an example from this extract. Indicate the type of writing where syllepsis of this kind would be quite out of place.

28. Learn by heart the first paragraph.

29. "What is the use of ideals?" asked the hard-headed man of business. "This world is a place where we have to deal with facts, not with dreams. There's no room for empty sentiment. Your idealist is a mere visionary, fond of talking, but incapable of doing anything effective."

Write your reply in a paragraph beginning: "'Well,' I answered, 'there may appear to be some truth in your objection; but . . .'"

No. XXV

1. Taking a turn the other day in the Abbey, I was struck with the affected attitude of a figure, which I do not remember to have seen before, and which upon exam-

ination proved to be a whole-length of the celebrated **Mr.**
5 Garrick.   Though I would not go so far with some good
Catholics abroad as to shut players altogether out of
consecrated ground, yet I own I was not a little scandalized
at the introduction of theatrical airs and gestures into a
place set apart to remind us of the saddest realities.
10 Going nearer, I found inscribed under this harlequin
figure the following lines:

> To paint fair Nature by divine command,
> Her magic pencil in his glowing hand,
15 A Shakespeare rose: then, to expand his fame
> Wide o'er this breathing world, a Garrick came.
> Though sunk in death the forms the Poet drew,
> The Actor's genius bade them breathe anew;
> Though, like the bard himself, in night they lay,
20 Immortal Garrick call'd them back to day:
> And till Eternity with power sublime
> Shall mark the mortal hour of hoary Time,
> Shakespeare and Garrick like twin-stars shall shine,
> And earth irradiate with a beam divine.

2. It would be an insult to my readers' understandings
25 to attempt anything like a criticism of this farrago of false
thoughts and nonsense.   But the reflection it led me into
was a kind of wonder, how, from the day of the actor here
celebrated to our own, it should have been the fashion to
compliment every performer in his turn that has had the
30 luck to please the town in any of the great characters of
Shakespeare, with the notion of possessing a *mind congenial with the poet's:* how people should come thus
unaccountably to confound the power of originating
poetical images and conceptions with the faculty of being
35 able to read or recite the same when put into words;
or what connection that absolute mastery over the heart
and soul of man, which a great dramatic poet possesses,
has with those low tricks upon the eye and ear, which a
player by observing a few general effects, which some

common passion, as grief, anger, etc., usually has upon 40
the gestures and exterior, can so easily compass.   To know
the internal workings and movements of a great mind,
of an Othello or a Hamlet for instance, the *when* and the
why and the *how far* they should be moved; to what
pitch a passion is becoming; to give the reins and to pull 45
in the curb exactly at the moment when the drawing in
or the slackening is most graceful; seems to demand a
reach of intellect of a vastly different extent from that
which is employed upon the bare imitation of the signs of
these passions in the countenance or gesture, which signs 50
are usually observed to be most lively and emphatic in
the weaker sort of minds, and which signs can, after all,
but indicate some passion, as I said before, anger, or grief,
generally; but of the motives and grounds of the passion,
wherein it differs from the same passion in low and vulgar 55
natures, of these the actor can give no more idea by his
face or gesture than the eye (without a metaphor) can
speak, or the muscles utter intelligible sounds.   But such
is the instantaneous nature of the impressions which
we take in at the eye and ear at a playhouse, compared 60
with the slow apprehension oftentimes of the understanding in reading, that we are apt not only to sink the
play-writer in the consideration which we pay to the actor,
but even to identify in our mind, in a perverse manner, the
actor with the character which he represents.   It is difficult 65
for a frequent playgoer to disembarrass the idea of Hamlet
from the person and voice of Mr. K.   We speak of Lady
Macbeth, while we are in reality thinking of Mrs. S.   Nor
is this confusion incidental alone to unlettered persons
who, not possessing the advantage of reading, are 70
necessarily dependent upon the stage-player for all the
pleasure which they can receive from the drama, and to
whom the very idea of *what an author is* cannot be made
comprehensible without some pain and perplexity of mind:
the error is one from which persons otherwise not meanly 75
lettered, find it almost impossible to extricate themselves.

3. Never let me be so ungrateful as to forget the very high degree of satisfaction which I received some years back from seeing for the first time a tragedy of Shakespeare performed, in which these two great performers sustained the principal parts. It seemed to embody and realize conceptions which had hitherto assumed no distinct shape. But dearly do we pay all our life after for this juvenile pleasure, this sense of distinctness. When the novelty is past, we find to our cost that instead of realizing an idea, we have only materialized and brought down a fine vision to the standard of flesh and blood. We have let go a dream, in quest of an unattainable substance.

4. How cruelly this operates upon the mind, to have its free conceptions thus cramped and pressed down to the measure of a strait-lacing actuality, may be judged from that delightful sensation of freshness, with which we turn to those plays of Shakespeare which have escaped being performed, and to those passages in the acting plays of the same writer which have happily been left out in performance. How far the very custom of hearing anything *spouted*, withers and blows upon a fine passage, may be seen in those speeches from Henry the Fifth, etc., which are current in the mouths of schoolboys from their being found in *Enfield Speakers*, and such kind of books. I confess myself utterly unable to appreciate that celebrated soliloquy in *Hamlet*, beginning "To be or not to be," or to tell whether it be good, bad, or indifferent, it has been so handled and pawed about by declamatory boys and men, and torn so inhumanely from its living place and principle of continuity in the play, till it is become to me a perfect dead member.

5. It may seem a paradox, but I cannot help being of opinion that the plays of Shakespeare are less calculated for performance on a stage, than those of almost any other dramatist whatever. Their distinguished excellence is a reason that they should be so.   There is so much in them, which comes not under the province of acting, with which eye, and tone, and gesture, have nothing to do.

CHARLES LAMB

QUESTIONS

1. Give a title to the extract.
2. Give titles to the paragraphs.
3. Considering the whole extract, what do you think is the most important thing in the first paragraph? Why?
4. What adjectives in the first paragraph indicate Lamb's disapproval of Garrick's statue?
5. With what are "saddest realities" contrasted?
6. Give in twelve words the essential idea of the lines of verse.
7. What is there false and nonsensical in the lines of verse?
8. What statement in the second paragraph best indicates the central idea of the paragraph?
9. Omitting the first sentence of the second paragraph we may divide the paragraph into four sections; thus—
    (a) Lamb wonders at a certain phenomenon.
    (b) The reason for Lamb's wonder.
    (c) The explanation of the phenomenon.
    (d) The phenomenon is common.
    Show where these sections begin and end.
10. "Lamb wonders at the . . . paid to the . . . at the expense of the . . ." Supply one word for each of the blanks.
11. What are the two characteristics of the great dramatic poet as indicated by Lamb?
12. What are the two characteristics of the actor as indicated by Lamb? Each characteristic (in No. 12) can be named in one word.
13. (a) Why are the words "of a great mind" (l. 42) important for Lamb's argument?
    (b) On what passage in the paragraph is your answer based?
14. What relation does the passage "the when and the why

. . . most graceful" (ll. 43–47) bear to the opening part of the sentence?

15. Why is the parenthesis "without a metaphor" (l. 57) necessary?

16. What, from the actor's point of view, is the important difference between the passions of "a great mind" and the passions of "the weaker sort of minds"?

17. Write out two sentences in the second paragraph which illustrate, but do not advance, the argument.

18. Substitute for "otherwise" (l. 75) a phrase that will bring out the full significance of the word in this context.

19. "Persons otherwise not meanly lettered." Of whom, in particular, is Lamb thinking? How do you know?

20. Why does Lamb call this sense of distinctions a "juvenile" pleasure?

21. (a) Write out any phrase in the second paragraph which corresponds to the "fine vision" in the third paragraph.

(b) Do the same with "the standard of flesh and blood."

22. What is the "novelty" of l. 84?

23. Summarize the fourth paragraph in ten words.

24. What phrases in the third paragraph correspond to "strait-lacing actuality"?

25. What word in the fourth paragraph is recalled by "torn so inhumanely . . . member"? (ll. 105–107.)

26. What relation does the last paragraph bear to the whole extract?

27. Why does it "seem a paradox" (l. 108)?

28. What is the "distinguished excellence" of Shakespeare's plays?

29. Learn by heart the last paragraph.

30. Give the derivation and meaning (in this extract) of harlequin, farrago, congenial, compass, incidental, perplexity, conceptions, appreciate, soliloquy, declamatory.

31. "One September night in 1811, Charles Lamb, having written an article on Shakespeare's tragedies inspired by his first sight of Garrick's statue in Westminster Abbey, bade his sister Mary good night and retired to bed. It was a dark, gusty night, and for a long time Charles lay awake listening to the wind tapping at his window.

In the early hours of the morning he dropped asleep and dreamed. He dreamed that he was in the Abbey at night-time, unaccountably left behind and locked in. And he found himself reading aloud in a low voice that went whispering among the statues the last sentences of his article on Shakespeare's tragedies. As his voice died away he heard a hoarse chuckle, and looking up into the shadows he saw the statue of Garrick move. Then it spoke."

Add another paragraph showing what the statue of Garrick had to say in reply to Lamb's article.

No. XXVI

1. A dispute has for some time divided the philosophers of Europe; it is debated whether Arts and Sciences are more serviceable or prejudicial to mankind. They who maintain the cause of literature, endeavor to prove their usefulness from the impossibility of a large number 5 of men subsisting in a small tract of country without them; from the pleasure which attends the acquisition; and from the influence of knowledge in promoting practical morality.

2. They who maintain the opposite opinion, display the 10 happiness and innocence of those uncultivated nations who live without learning; urge the numerous vices which are to be found only in polished society, enlarge upon the oppression, the cruelty, and the blood which must necessarily be shed, in order to cement civil society, and insist 15 upon the happy equality of conditions in a barbarous state preferable to the unnatural subordination of a more refined constitution.

3. This dispute, which has already given so much em-

20 ployment to speculative indolence, has been managed with
much ardor, and (not to suppress our sentiments) with
but little sagacity. They who insist that the sciences are
useful in *refined* society are certainly right, and they who
maintain that *barbarous* nations are more happy without
25 them, are right also. But when one side for this reason
attempts to prove them as universally useful to the
solitary barbarian as to the native of a crowded commonwealth; or, when the other endeavors to banish them as
prejudicial to all society, even from populous states as
30 well as from the inhabitants of the wilderness, they are
both wrong; since that knowledge which makes the
happiness of a refined European would be a torment to
the precarious tenant of an Asiatic wild.

4. Let me, to prove this, transport the imagination for
35 a moment to the midst of a forest in Siberia. There we
behold the inhabitant, poor indeed, but equally fond of
happiness with the most refined philosopher of China.
The earth lies uncultivated and uninhabited for miles
around him; his little family and he the sole and undis-
40 puted possessors. In such circumstances Nature and
Reason will induce him to prefer a hunter's life to that of
cultivating the earth. He will certainly adhere to that
manner of living which is carried on at the smallest expense of labor, and that food which is most agreeable to
45 the appetite; he will prefer indolent though precarious
luxury to a laborious though permanent competence,
and a knowledge of his own happiness will determine him
to persevere in native barbarity.

5. In like manner his happiness will incline him to bind
50 himself by no law. Laws are made in order to secure
present property, but he is possessed of no property which
he is afraid to lose, and desires no more than will be
sufficient to sustain him; to enter into compacts with
others would be undergoing a voluntary obligation without

the expectance of any reward. He and his countrymen 55
are tenants, not rivals, in the same inexhaustible forest;
the increased possessions of one by no means diminishes
the expectations arising from equal assiduity in another;
there are no need of laws, therefore, to repress ambition,
where there can be no mischief attending its most boundless 60
gratifications.

6. Our solitary Siberian will, in like manner, find the
sciences not only entirely useless in directing his practice,
but disgusting even in speculation. In every contemplation our curiosity must be first excited by the *appearances* 65
of things, before our reason undergoes the fatigue of
investigating the *causes*. Some of those appearances are
produced by experiment, others by minute inquiry;
some arise from a knowledge of foreign climates, and
others from an intimate study of our own. But there 70
are few objects in comparison which present themselves
to the inhabitant of a barbarous country; the game
he hunts, or the transient cottage he builds, make up
the chief objects of his concern; his curiosity, therefore, must be proportionably less; and if that is 75
diminished, the reasoning faculty will be diminished in
proportion.

7. Besides, sensual enjoyment adds wings to curiosity.
We consider few objects with ardent attention, but those
which have some connection with our wishes, our pleasures, 80
or our necessities. A desire of enjoyment first interests
our passions in the pursuit, points out the object of investigation, and Reason then comments where Sense has
led the way. An increase in the number of our enjoyments,
therefore, necessarily produces an increase of scientific 85
research; but in countries where almost every enjoyment
is wanting, Reason there seems destitute of its great inspirer, and speculation is the business of fools, when it
becomes its own reward.

90   8. The barbarous Siberian is too wise, therefore, to
exhaust his time in quest of knowledge, which neither
curiosity prompts, nor pleasure impels him to pursue.
When told of the exact admeasurement of a degree upon
the Equator at Quito, he feels no pleasure in the account;
95 when informed that such a discovery tends to promote
navigation and commerce, he finds himself no way interested in either.   A discovery, which some have pursued at
the hazard of their lives, affects him with neither astonishment nor pleasure.   He is satisfied with thoroughly
100 understanding the few objects which contribute to his own
felicity; he knows the properest places where to lay the
snare for the sable, and discerns the value of furs with
more than European sagacity.   More extended knowledge
would only serve to render him unhappy; it might lend
105 a ray to show him the misery of his situation, but could
not guide him in his efforts to avoid it.   Ignorance is the
happiness of the poor.

9. No, my friend, in order to make the sciences useful
in any country, it must first become populous; the in-
110 habitant must go through the different stages of hunter,
shepherd, and husbandman.   Then when property becomes valuable, and consequently gives cause for injustice;
then when laws are appointed to repress injury, and secure
possession; when men, by the sanction of those laws,
115 become possessed of superfluity; when luxury is thus
introduced and demands its continual supply, then it is
that the sciences become necessary and useful; the
State then cannot subsist without them; they must then
be introduced at once to teach men to draw the greatest
120 possible quantity of pleasure from circumscribed possession
and to restrain them within the bounds of moderate
enjoyment.

10. The sciences are not the cause of luxury, but its
consequence, and this destroyer thus brings with it an

antidote which resists the virulence of its own poison. 125
By asserting that luxury introduces the sciences, we assert
a truth; but if with those who reject the utility of learning
we assert that the sciences also introduce luxury, we shall
be at once false, absurd, and ridiculous.

OLIVER GOLDSMITH

QUESTIONS

1. Give a title to this essay.
2. Give titles to the paragraphs.
3. Divide the paragraphs into three groups, and justify your
   grouping.
4. (a) In the first paragraph is there any contrast implied
       between Arts and Sciences?
   (b) What single word in this paragraph is used to sum up
       both?
5. (a) What phrase in the second paragraph repeats the idea
       contained in the phrase "uncultivated nations"?
   (b) Find contrasting phrases in the same paragraph.
   (c) What word is contrasted with "equality"(l. 16)?
   (d) What word is contrasted with "barbarous" (l. 16)?
6. "Speculative indolence" (l. 20). Substitute for this
   phrase "people who ..." Supply words for the blank
   that will show that you fully understand Goldsmith's
   phrase.
7. How does the phrase "his little family . . . possessors"
   (l. 39) anticipate the following paragraph?
8. What is the relation between "He will certainly adhere
   . . . labor" (ll. 42–44) and the preceding sentence?
9. In l. 45 Goldsmith says, "He will prefer indolent though
   precarious luxury." Study the last paragraph of the
   essay, and bearing clearly in mind what Goldsmith's
   argument is, and for what purpose he has introduced the
   Siberian, criticize the sentence.
10. What is the key-sentence of the fifth paragraph?
11. Why would "to enter into compacts with others" be

"undergoing a voluntary obligation without the expectance of any reward" (ll. 53–55)?

12. What is the essential function of law as indicated in the fifth paragraph?

13. Bind—compact—obligation—repress: what idea is common to these four words?

14. Why is "in the same inexhaustible forest" (l. 56) better than "in the same forest"? Study the context carefully for your answer.

15. What, for the purposes of Goldsmith's argument in the sixth paragraph, is the most fundamental sentence of the paragraph?

16. "Few objects in comparison" (l. 71). In comparison with what?

17. Reason and Sense are the key-words of the seventh paragraph. Put down in two columns all the words (or phrases) in this paragraph which are connected in thought with these words. Thus "sensual enjoyment" is connected with "sense."

18. In the seventh paragraph the second sentence does not advance the argument; it merely elaborates the idea expressed in the first sentence of the paragraph. Show that this is so by writing out the words and phrases in this sentence which correspond to (a) sensual enjoyment, (b) wings, (c) curiosity.

19. What is the "great inspirer" (l. 87)?

20. Reduce the eighth paragraph to a series of notes; thus— "The Siberian and the pursuit of knowledge—no curiosity —no pleasure." Now continue.

21. Complete the following, "and speculation is the business of wise men, only when . . ." in such a way that it can be substituted in the paragraph for the original, and will show that you understand Goldsmith's argument (l. 88).

22. What word in the first sentence of the eighth paragraph marks a sharp contrast between that sentence and the one that precedes it?

23. Show that the eighth paragraph takes us back in thought to the sixth paragraph, as well as to the seventh.

24. In the eighth paragraph there is a sentence A, followed immediately by two more sentences B and C. A states a

general truth; B and C give specific instances of this
truth. What are the sentences?

25. What is an aphorism? Quote a few from this essay.

26. What, for the purpose of Goldsmith's argument in the ninth
paragraph, is the essential difference between the hunter,
the shepherd, and the husbandman?

27. Explain the phrase "circumscribed possession" (l. 120).
By what is his possession circumscribed? With what
phrase in the fifth paragraph is it contrasted?

28. In the last paragraph—
   (a) What is the destroyer?
   (b) What is the antidote?
   (c) What is the poison?

29. Give the derivation and meaning (in this essay) of
acquisition, influence, precarious, competence, rivals,
assiduity, disgusting, passions, sense, virulence, sanction.

30. Learn by heart the seventh paragraph.

31. Summarize the second paragraph in twenty words.

32. "This dark-eyed gipsy, who never in his life had entered a
schoolroom or opened a book, enjoyed the happiness of
the ignorant."

   Continue the paragraph (eight or nine sentences, or
   longer) by expanding this idea.

No. XXVII

1. To complain of the age we live in, to murmur at the
present possessors of power, to lament the past, to conceive
extravagant hopes of the future, are the common dispositions of the greatest part of mankind; indeed, the   *frivolity*
necessary effects of the ignorance and levity of the vulgar. 5
Such complaints and humors have existed in all times;
yet as all times have *not* been alike, true political sagacity
manifests itself in distinguishing that complaint which
only characterizes the general infirmity of human nature,
from those which are symptoms of the particular dis- 10
temperature of our own air and season.

2. Nobody, I believe, will consider it merely as the
language of spleen or disappointment, if I say that there
is something particularly alarming in the present con-
15 juncture. There is hardly a man, in or out of power, who
holds any other language. That government is at once
dreaded and condemned; that the laws are despoiled of
all their respected and salutary terrors; that their inaction
is a subject of ridicule, and their exertion of abhorrence;
20 that rank, and office, and title, and all the solemn plausi-
bilities of the world, have lost their reverence and effect;
that our foreign politics are as much deranged as our
domestic economy; that our dependencies are slackened
in their affection, and loosened from their obedience;
25 that we know neither how to yield nor how to enforce;
that hardly anything above or below, abroad or at home,
is sound and entire; but that disconnection and confusion,
in offices, in parties, in families, in parliament, in the
nation, prevail beyond the disorders of any former time:
30 these are facts universally admitted and lamented.

3. This state of things is the more extraordinary because
the great parties which formerly divided and agitated the
kingdom are known to be in a manner entirely dissolved.
No great external calamity has visited the nation; no
35 pestilence or famine. We do not labor at present under
any scheme of taxation new or oppressive in the quantity
or in the mode. Nor are we engaged in unsuccessful war,
in which our misfortunes might easily pervert our judgment; and our minds, sore from the loss of national glory,
40 might feel every blow of fortune as a crime in government.

4. It is impossible that the cause of this strange dis-
temper should not sometimes become a subject of discourse. It is a compliment due, and which I willingly pay,
to those who administer our affairs, to take notice in the
45 first place of their speculation. Our ministers are of
opinion that the increase of our trade and manufactures,

that our growth by colonization, and by conquest, have concurred to accumulate immense wealth in the hands of some individuals; and this again being dispersed among the people, has rendered them universally proud, ferocious, and ungovernable; that the insolence of some from their enormous wealth, and the boldness of others from a guilty poverty, have rendered them capable of the most atrocious attempts; so that they have trampled upon all subordination, and violently borne down the unarmed laws of a free government; barriers too feeble against the fury of a populace so fierce and licentious as ours. They contend that no adequate provocation has been given for so spreading a discontent; our affairs having been conducted throughout with remarkable temper and consummate wisdom. The wicked industry of some libelers, joined to the intrigues of a few disappointed politicians, have, in their opinions, been able to produce this unnatural ferment in the nation.

5. Nothing indeed can be more unnatural than the present convulsions of this country, if the above account be a true one. I confess I shall assent to it with great reluctance, and only on the compulsion of the clearest and firmest proofs; because their account resolves itself into this short but discouraging proposition, "That we have a very good ministry, but that we are a very bad people"; that we set ourselves to bite the hand that feeds us; that with a malignant insanity we oppose the measures, and ungratefully vilify the persons, of those whose sole object is our own peace and prosperity. If a few puny libelers, acting under a knot of factious politicians without virtue, parts, or character (such they are constantly represented by these gentlemen), are sufficient to excite this disturbance, very perverse must be the disposition of that people, amongst whom such a disturbance can be excited by such means. It is, besides, to no small aggravation of the public misfortune, that the disease, on this hypothesis,

appears to be without remedy. If the wealth of the nation
be the cause of its turbulence, I imagine it is not proposed
85 to introduce poverty as a constable to keep the peace.
If our dominions abroad are the roots which feed all this
rank luxuriance of sedition, it is not intended to cut them
off in order to famish the fruit. If our liberty has enfeebled
the executive power, there is no design, I hope, to call in
90 the aid of despotism to fill up the deficiencies of law.
Whatever may be intended, these things are not yet
professed. We seem, therefore, to be driven to absolute
despair; for we have no other materials to work upon,
but those out of which God has been pleased to form the
95 inhabitants of this island. If these be radically and essentially vicious, all that can be said is, that those men are
very unhappy, to whose fortune or duty it falls to administer the affairs of this untoward people. I hear it
indeed sometimes asserted, that a steady perseverance
100 in the present measures, and a rigorous punishment of
those who oppose them, will in course of time infallibly
put an end to these disorders. But this, in my opinion, is
said without much observation of our present disposition,
and without any knowledge at all of the general nature of
105 mankind. If the matter of which this nation is composed
be so very fermentable as these gentlemen describe it,
leaven never will be wanting to work it up, as long as
discontent, revenge, and ambition, have existence in the
world. Particular punishments are the cure for accidental
110 distempers in the state; they inflame rather than allay
those heats which arise from the settled mismanagement
of the government, or from a natural indisposition in the
people. It is of the utmost moment not to make mistakes
in the use of strong measures: and firmness is then only
115 a virtue when it accompanies the most perfect wisdom.
In truth, inconstancy is a sort of natural corrective of
folly and ignorance.

EDMUND BURKE

QUESTIONS

1. Give a title to this extract.
2. Give titles to the paragraphs.
3. Considering the extract as a whole, what do you regard as the most important statement in the first paragraph?
4. What phrase in the first paragraph practically repeats the idea of the phrase "the common dispositions of the greatest part of mankind"?
5. What does Burke mean by "the particular distemperature of our own air and season"? *our own time*
6. Why is "symptom" an appropriate word to use in connection with "distemperature"? *disease*
7. (a) What passage balances "characterizes the general infirmity of human nature"?
   (b) Show that it is a four-fold balance.
8. What is the key-phrase of the second paragraph?
9. "There is hardly a man, in or out of power, who holds any other language." Where else in this paragraph is the same idea expressed?
10. What single noun sums up the passage "That government *confusion* is . . . former time" (ll. 16–29)? (There is a noun in this passage which will answer the question.) *disconnection*
11. Back to what phrase (of eleven words) in the first paragraph does the second paragraph take us?
12. What does Burke mean by
    (a) solemn plausibilities (l. 20)? *institutions in society*
    (c) in offices (l. 28)? *positions of authority, government*
13. Why are the terrors of the law "salutary"?
14. What is the key-word of the third paragraph? *extraordinary*
15. In what way does the third paragraph contribute to the extract?
16. What is the relation in thought between the clauses "in which our misfortunes . . . judgment" and "our minds . . . government" (ll. 38–40)? *both results of an unsuccessful war*
17. Express the idea contained in "might . . . government," in other words using the word "responsible."
18. What is the key-sentence of the fourth paragraph?
19. The causes of the present discontents as given by the

ministers may be epitomized thus: "Increase in . . . *economu* and resulting . . . , aided by . . ." Supply one word for each blank.

20. A compliment is defined in the *Pocket Oxford Dictionary* as a "polite expression or implication of praise." Consider the word as used in l. 43, and make any comment that is suggested to you by the context.

21. Speculation (l. 45) as to what? *theories on discontent, dislocation*

22. What does Burke mean by "a guilty poverty" (l. 52)?

23. What does Burke mean by "temper" (l. 60)?

24. (a) What is the relation of the fifth paragraph to the fourth? *ministers ideas → Burkes ideas*

    (b) What word serves to emphasize the link? *More*

25. Quote one sentence from the fifth paragraph that elaborates the word "unnatural" (l. 65).

26. The fifth paragraph may be divided thus:

    (a) What is implied in the official explanation of the present discontent?

    (b) This explanation criticized.

    (c) Proposed official action and its criticism.

    Show where these sections begin and end.

27. There are seven conditional "if" clauses in the fifth paragraph. These seven hypotheses appear in the fourth paragraph as statements or implications of fact on the part of the government.

    Show that this is so by putting the hypotheses in one column, and in the other just those portions of the fourth paragraph to which they take us back in thought. Thus—

    (1) If the above account   (1) "Our ministers are of
        be a true one.   opinion . . ." to the
                                          end of the paragraph.

28. What unnatural correctives have been suggested in this last paragraph?

29. Why is "leaven" an appropriate word in l. 107?

30. With what are "accidental distempers" (l. 109) contrasted?

31. Show that in the passage "It is of the utmost moment . . . wisdom" (ll. 113–115) we have the figure of speech known as chiasmus. Try to reshape the sentence so as to get rid of chiasmus, keeping Burke's phraseology as far as

possible. What idea in Burke's sentence is emphasized by means of chiasmus?

32. Summarize in fifty words the passage "I hear it indeed . . . ignorance" (ll. 98–end).

33. Explain what Burke means by the last sentence of the extract.

34. Give the derivation and meaning (in this extract) of levity, humors, conjuncture, salutary, deranged, individuals (note carefully the use of this word. How is it illustrated here?), malignant, vilify, factious, parts, perverse, hypothesis, radically, aggravation, untoward.

35. Learn by heart the second paragraph.

36. Write a paragraph of which the following sentence gives the key: "The approach of the General Election in 1929 threw the country into a state of excitement."